Rescued!

EXPERIENCING THE REALITY OF GOD'S POWER

LEROY LAWSON

STANDARD PUBLISHING
Cincinnati, Ohio

All Scripture quotations, unless otherwise indicated, are taken from the HOLY BIBLE, NEW INTERNATIONAL VERSION®. NIV®. Copyright ©1973, 1978, 1984 by International Bible Society. Used by permission of Zondervan Publishing House. All rights reserved.

ISBN 0-7847-7129-4

Edited by Theresa C. Hayes
Cover design by DesignTeam
Inside design by Robert E. Korth

Standard Publishing, Cincinnati, OH
A division of Standex International Corporation.
©2001 by Standard Publishing.
All rights reserved.
Printed in the United States of America.

CONTENTS

1. Rescued From the Flood — 5
2. Rescued From the Enemy — 17
3. Rescued From Poverty — 31
4. Rescued From Unbelievers — 45
5. Rescued From the Impossible — 59
6. Rescued From a Fiery Furnace — 73
7. Rescued From a Wicked Plot — 87
8. Rescued From Fear — 101
9. Rescued From Sin — 115
10. Rescued From Death — 129

1
RESCUED FROM
THE FLOOD

Genesis 6:1–9:17

WHEN YOU ARE SITTING on the verandah overlooking the Pacific Ocean, admiring the brilliant blues and greens broken by delicate whitecaps and the sails of varied hues skipping across them, it's a little difficult to envision the grays and gales of Noah's flood.

I'm in Hawaii as I write, on Maui, looking out toward the horizon beyond the north shore, drinking in a panorama of such splendor my vocabulary fails me. I've come here with Brian, our windsurfing adopted son. He has tried his best to convert me to the sport of his passion, but I won't give in. I tried it here one year, just a bit to the east of this place, but the wind was overpowering and the constant uphauling of water-filled sails robbed me of any pleasure in this so-called *recreational* activity. Some athletic undertakings yield more reward in the spectating than in the participating—at least after you've turned sixty.

But today, with the sun shimmering in reflected glory on the waters, the windsurfers returning to the lawn dripping with achievement and, after a moment's respite, eagerly heading back to the chase, it could be tempting. Brian calls this stretch of beach "Disneyland for Adults." He swears he will never be content to be separated for long from this aquatic playland.

Water. If you grew up beside the ocean as I did, you are

never completely content away from it. Even after twenty years of desert living in Arizona, I still need an occasional marine fix.

It's hard to remember, as I meditate here today, that the ocean affording such delight to these windsurfers can be a destructive villain that wipes out cities, capsizes great ships, and every year feeds on countless human lives. But neither can I totally forget. No native of my part of the Oregon coast takes the sea lightly. We've seen the wrecked hulls, attended the sailors' funerals, and watched in fascination while the waves and the wind rearrange the shoreline at will. In my home county the sea ate a complete town in the days of my childhood.

Even we Oregonians, though, have never seen anything like Noah's flood. Only eight people survived to tell the story. It had to appear to the desperate doomed that God's loosened wrath had all humanity writhing beneath His ire.

The story in Genesis 6–9 doesn't begin with a great storm but in a great sorrow. *The Lord saw how great man's wickedness on the earth had become, and that every inclination of the thoughts of his heart was only evil all the time. The Lord was grieved that he had made man on the earth, and his heart was filled with pain.*

How far the human race has fallen in the Bible's five short opening chapters. When God created the heavens and the earth He took measure of His work and announced, *"It is good."* But by chapter 6 His creation is up to no good. One would be hard put to find a better definition of total depravity than this one: *every inclination of the thoughts of his heart was only evil all the time.* No softening of the indictment, no qualifying phrases, no extenuating circumstances, no redeeming qualities. Evil has taken charge.

An anguished creator prepares to throw away His creation as an artisan tosses his first experiments. He will eliminate the human race—and not just men and women, but their fellow creatures as well. As far as God is concerned, creation has misfired. He grieves.

This would be the end of the story, Genesis reports, except for what God does through Noah. *But Noah found favor in the eyes of the Lord. This is the account of Noah. Noah was a righteous man, blameless among the people of his time, and he walked with God.* How we'd like to know what this righteousness consisted of then, what it meant in the beginning to walk with God, and how it was even possible for one man to be so different from his fellows.

The eleventh verse gives us a hint: *Now the earth was corrupt in God's sight and was full of violence. God saw how corrupt the earth had become, for all the people on earth had corrupted their ways.* Corrupt. Violent. Far from the ideal God had in mind when He breathed life into clay. Noah, by contrast, lived peaceably with his neighbors. He did not participate in their decadence.

From genesis to degeneracy, from goodness to corruption in all their ways. What a sad (but not necessarily unique) tribal history.

A situation desperate—but not hopeless—because of what God chose to do through Noah.

So, as we sang in Sunday school about another storm, "The rains came down and the floods came up, the rains came down and the floods came up." Weeks, months Noah drifted in his homemade ark with his family and menagerie until finally the waters receded and the ark landed and God promised, *"Never again will all life be cut off by the waters of a flood; never again will there be a flood to destroy the earth."* And God said, *"This is the sign of the covenant I am making between me and you and every living creature with you, a covenant for all generations to come: I have set my rainbow in the clouds, and it will be the sign of the covenant between me and the earth. Whenever I bring clouds over the earth and the rainbow appears in the clouds, I will remember my covenant between me and you and all living creatures of every kind. Never again will the waters become a flood to destroy all life."*

It is one of the most remarkable rescues ever recorded.

8 *Rescued!*

Even today, wherever you find Christians and Jews and Muslims, you'll hear about Noah and the terrible flood. The story lives on, its symbols borrowed by poets and peasants alike. Look at them:
- The flood. We'll return to it again.
- The covenant, God's gracious agreement with humanity.
- The ark, the vessel of salvation.
- Noah, man of courage and obedience.
- The dove, symbol of hope.
- The olive leaf, another symbol of hope and, of course, peace.
- An altar, for worship and thanksgiving.
- And the rainbow, sign of the everlasting covenant.

There is enough meaning in these symbols to fill a dissertation, certainly more than one brief chapter can treat with any justice. Read the list again. Review the story again. It's about a God thing, this story of Noah and the flood. And the God thing is grace.

It is easy to miss the grace in the story, especially if you concentrate, as I have been doing, on the sinfulness of the people, on the destructiveness of the storm, and even on the relative goodness of Noah. (Did he on the strength of his virtue alone merit their supernatural rescue? Was the whole family that good? Every one of them?) Could Noah's righteousness have sustained him, his family, and all the animals in the ark? Could he have made a rainbow, stopped the storm, initiated a contract with God? You can't read the story and conclude that Noah is somehow the hero here. No, it's God's doing all the way. And what He is demonstrating to and through Noah and his family we call grace.

Like other readers of the New Testament book of 1 Peter, my understanding of Noah's experience has been permanently infused with the interpretation Peter gives it. He is really the one who taught me to focus not so much on Noah's activities but on God's.

Peter (1 Peter 3:18-22) reaches way back to Noah—actually, back even before the flood—to discuss the patience of

God. With every reason to wipe out the human race, instead He saved eight persons through the water. Peter treats Noah's flood as a foreshadowing of baptism. He hastens to make clear that the water isn't doing the saving. And the saved ones aren't somehow through their works saving themselves. God is saving them by His grace. If any human work is involved in baptism, it is as the pledge of a good conscience toward God. But that's still not all there is to it. It's the resurrection of Jesus Christ that does the work. (Peter mentions Jesus' crucifixion in verse 18, an event so historically pivotal, so universal in its significance that it reaches back to Noah's day and forward to our own and beyond.) Clearly we are dealing with more than a flood here. We are looking at grace.

When we compare the Genesis story with Peter's sermon, we find several facts they have in common:

- Human corruption. We call it sin.
- Our helplessness to save ourselves. The difficulties are overwhelming.
- The solitariness of the saving experience. Noah and family—alone among all the human race. The sinner before a righteous God, alone. The candidate for baptism, alone. There is a way through, but it requires absolute faithfulness in the face of opposition and ridicule, and it requires personal action. No one else can take hold of God's grace for you. No one else can be baptized for you, or saved for you. Only you can grasp God's hand and let Him graciously pull you to safety.
- God's initiative in providing a way to be redeemed from sin.
- Implicit in both passages—courage. Noah's is obvious: courage in the face of his neighbors' taunts; courage when the rains were pounding and the waters were rising; courage when the confined days became weeks and months aboard a drifting ark; courage to start life over in a new place.

I can't read Peter's sermon without remembering what courage it required of me as a scared, teary-eyed but determined nine-year-old to walk to the front of his church to make his confession of faith and then submit to baptism. If the testimony of those I have baptized is to be taken seriously, mine was not the only response to God's invitation that required unaccustomed boldness.

In Noah's case, courage looks very much like patience. The writer of Hebrews says it was "holy fear" (11:7) that motivated Noah to construct his strange vessel in the face of his contemporaries' sneering. Fear is probably the right word, because Noah was afraid—more afraid of the disapproval of God than of the rejection of his neighbors. But when you consider the years the ark was under construction, and then the long, long boat ride, and the repeated tests of outside conditions with the raven and the dove, his courage looks very much like patience—a stubborn determination to keep going when there was precious little encouragement to do so. God was saving him, but what a long time it took!

Linger with me a little longer on Maui. It's another beautiful day. As a mainlander I can't help wondering whether these island dwellers ever tire of this surfeit of beauty. The wind is blowing a little lighter than yesterday; otherwise everything looks about the same. The lowering clouds hiding the top of the mountain across the waters to the west have changed little in the last twenty-four hours. I've been studying their formations, remembering them from earlier visits to Hawaii. The peak is usually invisible. Ordinarily the mountaintops here are swathed in clouds like heavenly armories storing fierce firepower for future storms. This is in the Pacific, after all, where from time to time winds of hurricane force rip across the island, forcing the trees to their knees, burying towns and terrifying people with their fury. It isn't any wonder that from antiquity island dwellers believed the gods made their dwelling places on mountaintops, where with lofty immunity they could survey the havoc they periodically wreaked below.

The other renters in our house are windsurfers. I'm the only holdout. I tell them I've been there, done that. I would rather participate in their happiness vicariously. They love the water and I love watching as they test their mettle against it.

I luxuriate here where the relaxed tempo of life makes it easy to forget the press of business on the mainland. For the moment, demanding schedules, ringing phones, and daily crises fade to the deep recesses of the mind. You almost forget that this paradise is Fantasy Island for us working stiffs. It's an interruption, a temporary diversion, a blip, nothing more. Next week the morning alarms will ring as always and the phone will tyrannize, as is its wont. I have to confess that if today some latter-day Noah were to start constructing an ark and warning his neighbors to prepare for the coming tsunami, this neighbor would stretch, yawn, and mumble, "Yeah, sure," unable to convince myself that God really intends that this bliss should end.

Yet if my neighbor pressed his case, and if I were honest, I would have to admit that God intended life to consist of more than feeding my lethargy and indulging my various physical urges. And though I would have a hard time pumping up any enthusiasm for day laboring on his ark-building crew, I would cast a wary eye to the cloudy mountaintop and scan the waters for multiplying whitecaps. He could just be right, my righteous neighbor. I wonder, you see, whether I would have taken the first Noah seriously, either. He was a man who feared God—and he wasn't casual about deep water, either. Whether he mused over the theological implications of salvation by water as he was pounding the gopher wood planks into place, I can't say. But we don't have to know. His actions tell the whole story. A storm was coming, and for reasons perhaps even Noah did not fully understand, God had let him in on the secret. He showed him how he could be saved, though all else would perish. As far as Noah was concerned, God was being gracious to him. And that was enough.

Frankly, I have sat through too many debates among budding theologians on the issue of whether we are saved by works or saved by grace. Ephesians 2:8, 9 insists *For it is by grace you have been saved, through faith—and this not from yourselves, it is the gift of God—not by works, so that no one can boast.* How can you argue with a statement as clear as this one? Yet James 2:24 counters, *You see that a person is justified by what he does and not by faith alone.* Equally clear, isn't it?

Noah's case is the indisputable proof that both are right. His faith in God is obvious. The grace of God is beyond doubting. And the work Noah does in response to the instructions of the gracious God he has faith in carried him over the waters to safety and new life.

I don't know whether it is still there or not, but eight or ten years ago there was a highway rest area on the South Carolina-Georgia border. There, near the shaded picnic tables where weary travelers take a break from their journeys to and fro, there's a sign that must have caused more than one reader to wonder what to do: "Rest Area," it reads. "No Loitering."

It makes you think, doesn't it? Is there such a thing as resting without loitering?

The answer is yes. This is really what grace offers: rest for the storm-tossed soul, serenity in the tempest, certainty in the confusion, peace in the battle, a presence in the loneliness, a lighted path through the darkness—an ark in the flood. Rest.

But no loitering. There is a boat to be built, a family to save, a host of animals to rescue. But not to worry. You can be at rest even as you toil. The blueprints are clear; building materials are available, and the deadline is reasonable. No loitering, but rest. By the grace of God, we shall be saved. By the labor of our hands, we are justified.

The story of Noah and the flood, in other words, is about grace, but not cheap grace. Columnist Barbara Reynolds commented on one of California's periodic earthquakes (several years ago *in USA Today*), that it might be "only in the eye of a storm or the epicenter of an earthquake" that you and I "understand that our happiness and security depend less on 'manpower' than on the grace of God." It seems as if the earth must come tumbling down and the floods must rise up around us before we turn back to the God we have ignored. You couldn't have convinced Noah that his happiness and security depended on his hands (and his sons'). The whole project was God's. If they were to be saved, and they believed they were to be, it was God's affair, not theirs. Theirs was but to build a boat. So their bodies labored, but their souls were at rest.

It's a good lesson to remember while relaxing on an ocean beach. Recreation, napping, entertainment, just vegging out—these all have the appearance of "rest," but looks can fool you. Genuine rest is not in either inactivity itself (call it recess, or a break, a holiday or vacation, or whatever) or even in strenuous activity you call recreation (which is what these windsurfers call what they are doing; it still looks like hard work to me).

John explains the source of rest (what Reynolds calls happiness and security) as something that comes from God:

Dear children, let us not love with words or tongue but with actions and in truth. This then is how we know that we belong to the truth, and how we set our hearts at rest in his presence whenever our hearts condemn us. For God is greater than our hearts, and he knows everything (1 John 3:18-21).

John recommends living so close to God that, in spite of the unrighteousness of which we know we are guilty *(our hearts condemn us),* we have the confidence that God doesn't condemn us. Therefore, no matter what we are doing, no matter how fierce the storm or deep the flood, our hearts are at rest. The source of our serenity is God, who is greater than our hearts. He knows everything but wants to save us anyway—just as He rescued Noah and his family, and through them the human race. Although Noah was "justified by what he did," as James would have it, it was, as the apostle Paul asserted, "by grace" he was saved.

14 Rescued!

GEAR UP

1. In what ways do you think the world in which Noah lived was similar to the world we live in today?

2. What made it possible for Noah to live righteously in the midst of the ungodly society that surrounded him?

3. "Righteousness" is simply doing right. How can a believer today do right when he is surrounded by unrighteousness?

4. In what areas are you most tempted to compromise righteousness with unrighteousness?

5. How does recognizing God's righteousness and holiness make you want to live a more righteous and holy life?

6. What does God's willingness to plot a rescue (that foreshadows His gift of salvation) tell you about His character?

7. Based on what you've read, what would you say was Noah's greatest need?

8. Would you say that Noah's acceptance of God's plan took courage? Explain your answer.

9. How does understanding God's character and Noah's need help you understand your own need of rescue from sin?

16 *Rescued!*

10. Noah was at peace during one of the most violent times in human history because he knew that God had a plan to save him from a dying world. Read the following verses. List evidences of serenity we should display because Jesus seeks to rescue us. Matthew 6:25-34; 11:28-30; John 14:25-27; 1 Peter 5:6, 7

11. Are you lacking peace in any of the areas mentioned in the verses listed above? Which one(s)? How can that peace be restored?

12. Although God's plan for his family's salvation gave Noah peace, Noah did not "loiter." He picked up a hammer and saw and completed the structure God commanded him to build! Read the following verses. What faithful actions of ours complete our ark of rescue? Philippians 2:12-15; 1 Thessalonians 5:16-18; 2 Timothy 3:16, 17; Hebrews 10:25

13. Are you "loitering" in any of the areas mentioned in the Scriptures listed above? Which one(s)? Decide to take a specific action this coming week to *continue to work out your salvation with fear and trembling* (Philippians 2:12).

2
RESCUED FROM
THE ENEMY

Judges 7:1-25

GIDEON'S STORY is one of the strangest in the Bible, yet perhaps one of the most helpful. If it has been a while since you read this unusual account, stop and review it now before reading farther in this chapter. It will still seem a pretty unorthodox way to conduct a military campaign, but as a study of how God comes to the rescue, it's one of the best. You'll find several principles that you'll want to recall the next time you are up against seemingly overwhelming odds.

Here is the first one:

God does His best work against overpowering forces.

"You have too many men <u>for me</u> to deliver Midian into their hands. In order that Israel <u>may not boast against me that her own strength</u> has saved her, . . ."

Look at the words carefully. This story is not really about Gideon at all, except as the instrument God chooses for rescuing Israel. *You have too many men <u>for me</u> to deliver Midian into their hands.* God wants Gideon—and all his people—to understand where the real power is coming from in this contest. The greater the odds against Gideon, the more convincing is God's case.

When America went to war in the Arabian Gulf in the early nineties, President Bush, chairman of the Joint Chiefs of Staff General Powell, and General Schwarzkopf led our nation in one of our most carefully calculated battles in our history. Every precaution was taken to be certain American forces would not be at risk. The buildup of men and material was enormous and ultimately indomitable. The war was over in days. American might was proved once again. Not much was said about God's role in the war. American ingenuity and massive arms prevailed.

Historian Barbara Tuchman might not have been too impressed, though. She believes that in the final analysis war is "the unfolding of miscalculations." Wars are won or lost mostly by mistakes, she insists. To listen to the ongoing debate about the Persian Gulf War, we wonder whether Professor Tuchman isn't right. Should the president have called a halt to the hostilities when he did? Wouldn't it have been better to fight on until President Hussein was either killed or captured? Aren't things as bad in the Middle East now, or even worse, than before the war? What exactly did America win? Did our calculations prove to be *mis*calculations after all?

At church one Sunday someone handed me a clipping, undoubtedly someone who had been studying me and had come to a similar conclusion about my style of leadership. "Miscalculations on a personal level can be just as devastating as miscalculations on an international level," the unknown author writes. "It is not the *mis* in miscalculating that is the problem; it is the calculating. When we operate out of a belief system that says that we should be able to understand everything and that when we do we can control everything, we are in big trouble."

God seems to be giving Gideon a similar lesson, doesn't He? God will see to it that Gideon is victorious, but he must not believe that his coming victory over the Midianites can be attributed to his brilliant strategy and tactics, or to the superior numbers and fighting skill of the Israelites. Any student of military history in the future would quickly conclude that Gideon's was one of the most freakish victories of all time. Here, centuries before the apostle Paul, God was telling Gideon what He would later reveal to Paul, *"My grace is sufficient for you, for my power is made perfect in weakness"* (2 Corinthians 12:9). A handful of ill-equipped soldiers going up against the powerful Midian army—and winning? It can only be said, "To God be the glory."

Most of us will not have Gideon's military experience, but in other ways large and small we have learned something of God's all-sufficient grace. What experienced Christian does not know what it is to have his or her inadequacies miraculously overcome? Julian Smith provides a good example. When the San Diego resident saw television reports of the Oklahoma City bombing a few years ago, he strongly felt the Lord leading him there to help. He left home with only one hundred dollars and no prior arrangements. When he arrived, housing was provided. He immediately went to work in the intensive care unit of the hospital nearest the bombing site. He had no training for this service; he just did whatever he was asked to do. At the memorial service for victims he spent four hours hugging people.

He felt strong at the time, he said, but when he got home and tried to talk about his experience, he was overwhelmed with sobbing. He had given his all and more. What happened to him was not unlike Gideon's experience: "God opened doors and gave me power to serve him," Julian said. God's grace was sufficient to make up for his weakness.

I have written elsewhere at some length about this passage from 2 Corinthians. It summarizes my experience as a believer. All these years it has seemed I have had only weakness to offer, but God has never withheld His strength.

Gideon is about to learn the same wonderful lesson. He has nothing to fear: God does His best work against overpowering forces.

God's rescue is not for the fearful.

"Anyone who trembles with fear may turn back . . ."

Does it impress you that twenty-two thousand men were allowed to go home? Encouraged, even? My Bible concordance uses this passage as an example of cowardice. Is that fair? Were they cowardly or merely prudent? They were afraid, the verse says, but who wouldn't have been? What soldier preparing for a battle promising sure death wouldn't opt out if given the chance? It seems to this nonmilitary writer that the twenty-two thousand merely exercised reasonable caution. Gideon said they could go, so they went. I would have gone with them.

That left ten thousand. Still a respectable army. Were they all fearless? I doubt it. Some, maybe even most, were; the rest just weren't about to admit any nervousness. They were fighters, and they would fight!

Jimmy Carter says that the Carter Center in Atlanta, which monitors the world's wars, keeps tabs at any one time on one hundred ten of them scattered across the planet, an enormous number, it seems to me. Of these, about seventy erupt into violence each year, and of the seventy, thirty can be called major wars, claiming more than one thousand deaths on the battlefield. The center estimates that these days there are almost ten civilian deaths, including many women and children, for each soldier killed.

Today's media reports tend to concentrate on one or two of these at a time, Bosnia, for example, or wherever large numbers of American troops are involved. You can't blame the press; they can't do justice to so many conflicts simultaneously. But even in less-covered conflicts the monthly slaughter is immense.

What the media often overlook is that into each of these countries God's army of rescuers is also sent. Relief and development workers associated with well-known agencies like World Vision and Food for the Hungry, missionaries from a wide variety of denominations, and individuals convinced that the Lord has called them to alleviate human suffering work sacrificially to save as many lives as they can. In such situations, God's rescues are not for the fearful.

Don't expect the predictable from God.

"Separate those who lap the water with their tongues like a dog from those who kneel down to drink." Three hundred men lapped with their hands to their mouths. All the rest got down on their knees to drink. The Lord said to Gideon, "With the three hundred men that lapped I will save you and give the Midianites into your hands. Let all the other men go, each to his own place."

If you thought about it a week, would you ever come up with God's method of selecting His fighting men? The goal is to slash the fighting force to about a tenth of its original size. The first step is to dismiss the scared ones. That leaves about a third of the thirty-two thousand still with you. That's still nine thousand seven hundred too many. To get the number down to an acceptable three hundred, the Lord devises this crazy "dog-lapping" test.

Even as a boy in Sunday school I had trouble with this test. I couldn't imagine how the men could get enough to drink by lapping up the water. But then, I couldn't see how dogs pull it off, either. It seemed a most inefficient way to convey water from a bowl (or from their hands, in this case) to the stomach. Once again, I would have been eliminated.

Then these strangely selected warriors are armed—with trumpets and empty jars. As I said, you can't expect the predictable from God.

But this isn't a bad lesson to learn about the Lord, is it? American poet Randall Jarrell laments, "If I can think of it, it isn't what I want" (from his "Sick Child"). It is the unpredictable, the unthinkable, that draws us back to God, His refusal to stay put in our categories, to march to our tune, to marshal His troops according to the manual. If His ways were our ways, would we be interested in Him?

The Bible is a record of God's surprises. What, for example, do you think of the promised land? Place yourself in Abraham's shoes. Not Abraham the patriarch, but Abram the resident of Ur of the Chaldees in Mesopotamia, where with his countrymen he enjoyed springs of fresh water, abundant rains, green pastures and ripe cornfields, and well-fed sheep and cattle. Where did God call him? To the south. And what did he find there? Desert, little rainfall, poor pastureland, few springs, sparse population, and tough foraging for the sheep and cattle. I understand that some Jews and Canadians have joked that Moses misunderstood God. Moses thought He said Canaan, when God meant Canada! (I'd have opted for Oregon, although today I would have been certain He said Hawaii.)

What kind of God would choose a barren desert as a promised land? The same one who would go into battle with three hundred men armed with trumpets and jars!

Is it God's sense of humor, this penchant for the unexpected, or just His way of demonstrating His sovereignty? Who can't identify with Abraham Lincoln, who once confessed to Albert G. Hodges, "I claim not to have controlled events, but confess plainly that events have controlled me. Now, at the end of three years' struggle the nation's condition is not what either party, or any man devised, or expected. God alone can claim it." This sense of being overtaken by events beyond his control but not beyond God's was still with him in his second inaugural address, when he told an embattled nation, "With high hope for the future, no prediction in regard to it is ventured." He had learned the hardest possible way that he could not be sovereign in the events of the war. No one in the South or the North predicted that the protracted, bloody hostilities would still be going on.

To jump to the most surprising act of all: Who could have dreamed that God's final victory over Satan, sin, and death would be accomplished through an ignominious cross?

Don't expect the predictable from God.

Take your encouragement where you can find it.

During that night the Lord said to Gideon, "Get up, go down against the camp, because I am going to give it into your hands. If you are afraid to attack, go down to the camp with your servant Purah and listen to what they are saying. Afterward, you will be encouraged to attack the camp." So he and Purah his servant went down to the outposts of the camp.

"*If you are afraid to attack!*" God has just reduced Gideon's forces from thirty-two thousand to three hundred and armed them with trumpets and jars. *If you are afraid!*

C. S. Lewis wrote some helpful advice for the fearful in 1948, just three years after the atomic bombing of Hiroshima and Nagasaki that ended World War II. I'm just old enough to remember people seriously wondering how they were to exist in what they were already calling the Atomic Age. Humanity had never lived under an atomic cloud before. Lewis said he was tempted to tell them to live as they would have if this were the sixteenth century instead of the twentieth. Back then the plague traumatized London almost every year. Or they could live as they would have in the Viking age, when Scandinavians terrorized the British who went to bed thinking they could have their throats slit any night. What makes the threat of the atom bomb any more terrible? "You are already living in an age of cancer, an age of syphilis, an age of paralysis, an age of air raids, an age of railway accidents, an age of motor accidents." We could add to his list AIDS, airplanes, genocide, floods, earthquakes, road rage (with its drive-by shootings), gang attacks, and so on. Name your trouble—and tremble.

Lewis's point is that it is useless to whimper and mope "because the scientists have added one more chance of painful and premature death to a world which already bristled with such chances and in which death itself was not a chance at all, but a certainty." I like his prescription: "If we are going to be destroyed by an atomic bomb, let that bomb when it comes find us doing sensible and human things—

24 *Rescued!*

praying, working, teaching, reading, listening to music, bathing the children, playing tennis, chatting to our friends over a pint and a game of darts—not huddled together like frightened sheep and thinking about bombs."[1]

God's advice to Gideon is equally action-oriented: Get up and check out the enemy's camp. You'll see they are not as ferocious as you fear.

Gideon did what he was told. Eavesdropping, he learned of his enemy's belief that *"God has given the Midianites and the whole camp into* [Gideon's] *hands."* It was all he needed to hear. *He returned to the camp of Israel and called out, "Get up! The Lord has given the Midianite camp into your hands."*

Nothing has changed, really, except Gideon's perspective. He still has three hundred soldiers bearing ridiculous arms. The opposition is still awesome. But now Gideon has heard the word of the Lord and seen what the Lord sees. He is ready for battle.

The Lord's ways are not our ways.

Dividing the three hundred men into three companies, he placed trumpets and empty jars in the hands of all of them, with torches inside.

"Watch me," he told them. "Follow my lead. When I get to the edge of the camp, do exactly as I do. When I and all who are with me blow our trumpets, then from all around the camp blow yours and shout, 'For the Lord and for Gideon.'"

So the battle is joined and the weird tactics engaged. To read this passage is to appeal as the psalmist does, with renewed urgency, *Show me your ways, O Lord, teach me your paths; guide me in your truth and teach me, for you are God my Savior, and my hope is in you all day long* (25:4, 5) and to discover with Isaiah, *"For my thoughts are not your thoughts, neither are your ways my ways," declares the Lord* (55:8).

I have spent a lifetime trying to learn this lesson.

Recently I learned of another offbeat battle plan that

worked for the Americans in World War II. The Army's Twenty-third Headquarters Special Troops was a "camouflage unit" of a thousand artists, communications technicians, and combat engineers that moved through France, Belgium, and Luxembourg armed with—not trumpets and jars, but equally impotent weapons—life-sized inflatable rubber tanks, airplanes, and cannons. For a touch of realism, the men employed tape recordings of cursing soldiers and rumbling equipment, amplified by huge loudspeakers. To top off the illusion they employed canisters that exploded like real artillery.

In the dark the soldiers assumed the position of a real combat unit so the actual one could sneak into better position for outflanking the enemy—or grabbing a little rest. Who would have believed? Even more unbelievable—the ruse, beginning shortly after the D-day invasion in France, worked. Again and again the Germans, looking through field glasses at the phony unit from as little as a few hundred yards away, did not suspect that anything had changed. Not your normal expected military operation, but an effective one.

Reading through the Bible should convince the most stubborn skeptic that God majors in the unexpected. Would you have guessed the creator would wipe out His creation, as He did in Noah's time? Or select the descendants of Abraham to be the chosen people? Or arrange for His Son's nativity in a stable? Or rescue the human race through a cross? Or anoint the early church's most violent opponent to become its leading missionary? Or, I would have to add, use someone like me to proclaim the gospel?

Every time I visit the holy land I realize again that I just don't know how to second-guess God. Take Jerusalem, for example. It's not my idea of a holy city. It does not stand at the head of a great river. It has no harbor. It isn't even at the crossroads of important highways. It is away from the main trade routes. In addition, it has no attractive natural resources (unless you consider an excess of rocks to be one), and it has little strategic geographical importance in protecting any prized territory. Yet of this basically unattractive landscape Isaiah says, *The law will go out from Zion, the word of the Lord from Jerusalem* (2:3). Jerusalem is the holy city because God so decreed. That's reason enough.

God's ways are not our ways.

Yet His ways prevail.

I like the story Madeleine L'Engle tells of the child whose Sunday school teacher asked the class to draw pictures of Bible stories. This pupil drew a rectangle with four wheels, obviously a cart. In it were three stick figures, two passengers and a driver. It was this perceptive student's rendition of the story of the Garden of Eden. The third figure was God driving Adam and Eve out of the garden.

That's not what we usually understand the word "drive" to mean in its Genesis 3 context, but perhaps in this instance as in so many others a child should lead us. We concentrate on the tragedy of Adam and Eve's loss of paradise. The child is right, though. Even though they have to face the consequences of their sin, they are not forsaken. God is "driving" them. They will be safe. So will Gideon and his army.

When we are weak, still He is strong.

---

[1]Martindale, Wayne & Root, Jerry, eds. *The Quotable Lewis.* Wheaton: Tyndale House Publishers, 1989.

GEAR UP

1. What about you? Have you experienced a time when God used you in spite of—or perhaps because of—your weakness? What happened as a result?

2. With which group do you most identify; the twenty-two thousand who went home or the ten thousand who stayed? Explain your answer.

3. In what area of life are you most tempted to turn back?

4. Dr. Lawson asks this question about God: If His ways were our ways, would we be interested in Him? What is your answer? If God's ways were your ways, would you be interested in Him? Would you trust Him? Explain your answers.

5. Consider Dr. Lawson's statement, "The Bible is a record of God's surprises." What surprises have you found in God's Word?

6. In what ways has God surprised you in your life?

7. Consider Dr. Lawson's statement, "God majors in the unexpected." How have you discovered this to be true?

8. What difference did it make for Gideon to hear God's words and see what God saw?

9. Dr. Lawson writes, "Nothing has changed, really, except Gideon's perspective." If you were able to visualize the army of God prepared for each battle in your life, how might this change your perspective?

10. Instead of "nothing," isn't this change in perspective in fact, everything?

11. Read Psalm 144:1, 2. What did David say that God did for him?

12. Read Ephesians 6:10-14. What has God provided for our safety in our daily spiritual battles against Satan and the evil forces of darkness?

13. Go back now and reread the five principles that can help you when you face overwhelming circumstances. (Dr. Lawson outlined them under the five subheads in this chapter.) Underline the one that is most meaningful to you right now, then personalize it for your own heart. *(Example: God's rescue is not for the fearful, therefore I need to confess my fearfulness to Him and remember that His strength is sufficient for me.)*

3
RESCUED FROM
POVERTY
Ruth 1–4

ENTREAT ME NOT to leave thee, or to return from following after thee: for whither thou goest, I will go; and where thou lodgest, I will lodge: thy people shall be my people, and thy God my God: where thou diest, will I die, and there will I be buried: the Lord do so to me, and more also, if aught but death part thee and me (Ruth 1:16, 17, *KJV*).

No words better exemplify married love—the commitment, mutual sacrifices, and lifelong provision of husband for wife, wife for husband—than this familiar selection from the book of Ruth. We preachers routinely borrow Ruth's speech to enhance our wedding ceremonies. The words have been set to beautiful music.

When they hear this inspiring speech, however, few in attendance at the wedding are aware that the words were not originally spoken by a bride to a groom; Ruth is not speaking to her husband but to her mother-in-law!

The circumstances are far from romantic, also. With the deaths of their husbands, Naomi and her two daughters-in-law face a desperate situation. For their sakes, Naomi is urging the younger women to go back to their people, where they will be cared for. She is old and beyond marrying again and will only be in their way.

Orpah agrees, kisses her mother-in-law good-bye, takes

her leave, and that's the last we hear of her. Ruth can't bring herself to go; she is too attached to the older woman. No matter how bleak their future together, she promises she will not desert her.

The rest of the story is well-known. They return to Naomi's people, and in time Ruth marries their benefactor, Boaz.

It's not that love story which captures our interest right now, though. It's their rescue from poverty.

What it means to be poor

And poor they are. Reduced to eking out a living from other people's leftovers, they pluck whatever grain they can find. You've seen their kind, stooping beside the highway, fishing for stray bottles, scavenging through garbage dumps for something salvageable, rummaging through trash cans behind restaurants for something to quiet their rumbling stomachs. On Manila's Smokey Mountain twenty-five thousand men, women, and children pick their way through the refuse, saved from starvation by other people's castoffs. Along every highway and byway of India you'll find them, their one article of clothing hanging loosely from bony shoulders. You can't help noticing that India is a country of fat cows and thin people. In America the marginal poor are less obvious but present all too numerous, in city slums, in rural huts, in the shadows of prosperity. We see them, yet don't see them. They exist at the periphery of our lives, nameless rebukes to our thoughtless good luck.

Ruth's story grasps our attention in part because she, Orpah, and Naomi have names. They are real persons to us. They have not yet been reduced to such desperate straits as I describe above, but unless they act soon they will be.

If, as has been wisely said, poverty is not lack of money but rather lack of options, then Naomi and Ruth are twice poor. They have no money, and as women, they have precious few options.

What it means to be a poor woman

Naomi doesn't fool herself. As an Israelite in Moab, without a husband she is nobody. And even though Orpah and Ruth are Moabite women, their condition is not much better. Naomi urges them to return to their mothers' homes so that they'll be available for another marriage. Each needs a man in that man's world. She will go on alone to the land of her people.

Even in Judah, which is also a man's world, Naomi will legally be a nobody. She and Ruth must depend on Naomi's kinsman for succor. Her future looks dark; she is too old to remarry. She still believes in God—but she believes so strongly in His providence that she blames Him for her plight: *"Don't call me Naomi,"* she tells her kinsmen upon her return home. *"Call me Mara, because the Almighty has made my life very bitter. I went away full, but the Lord has brought me back empty. Why call me Naomi? The Lord has afflicted me; the Almighty has brought misfortune upon me."*

The precariousness of their lives is not overlooked in the story. Ruth is especially vulnerable. A single young woman, as Boaz's paternal attitude makes clear, needs protection.

Reading this account as a modern male reminds me that throughout human history men have been a threat to unattached women. Even in our so-called enlightened era, a single woman's lot is not an enviable one. Although I have grown pretty weary of the militancy and paranoia of today's women's lib movement, and sometimes find myself muttering, "The ladies do protest too much," I have to admit the justice in their cause. Revisiting Ruth is sobering. No political agenda motivates the author, no paranoia slants the truth. The tale is quietly told, the unadorned facts allowed to speak for themselves. But the facts are brutal. The gulf between men's rights and women's liberties is great and unbridgeable. Boaz is a good man and kind. Ruth is a virtuous woman who, at the urging of her mother-in-law, becomes somewhat manipulative in order to win the favor of Boaz. Without him, she will struggle indefinitely in hardship and danger. The woman's place leaves much to be desired.

Gender poverty, we could call her situation.

What it means to have limited ability

As I read the story I can't help thinking of another kind of poverty as well. The women have few skills to offer; their abilities are limited to tightly circumscribed roles, and those roles presume a husband. What can these single women do? Glean for a few grains. Seek a bare subsistence. Beg. No college education, no professional training, no job openings, almost no options. Certainly no such thing as equal opportunities.

This comes to mind because of a recent experience. In my younger days I received excellent advice. Go to college. Get a good education. Prepare yourself for the job market. Develop some marketable skills.

So I did. As a result, there are some things I can do with a fair degree of competence. I can talk. I can read and write. I can manage organizations, if they aren't too big or too complicated. Let's see, is there anything else? Not that I can think of.

There are some pretty important things I can't do, also. You don't want me fixing your appliances or mending your fence or, Heaven forbid, repairing your car. Unlike my father, who could figure out how to do anything with his hands, I am a doddering idiot regarding all things electronic or mechanical.

Hence my story.

At first blush there hardly seems to be any point of contact between the story of Ruth's rescue from abject poverty far from her homeland and my rescue by strangers far from home on the stretch of I-5 just south of Tracey, California. But bear with me while I tell my tale.

It was a crazy thing we were doing, anyway. Three months after my retirement from a twenty-year pastorate in Mesa, Arizona, Joy and I and our grandson Matt were driving north from Hope International University in Fullerton to the Pacific Northwest and our annual all-Lawson family vacation. What made this trip different is that we were pulling a trailer carrying a couple of motorcycles: a 1994 Shadow, once my prized possession but now the property of my son-in-law David; and a 1999 Harley Davidson Dyna-Glide Convertible, the bike of my dreams, which our former congregation had lovingly presented as my retirement gift. (What does it say about a church that these otherwise sensible people would give a Harley to their sixty-year-old preacher?)

We don't own a trailer, but the university does. Farrell Sparks, the school's jack-of-all-trades operations manager, wrestled the two bikes into the tiny trailer once used by our drama group, outfitted it with electric brakes, installed a trailer hitch on the school's ancient Town Car, and sent us on our way.

The trip wasn't exactly uneventful. After three hundred miles of not completely trouble-free driving, we broke down about seventy miles short of Sacramento, our first day's destination. When smoke filled the back seat of the car, it seemed the better part of wisdom to pull over. That's when we discovered the trail of transmission fluid behind, and the growing pool beneath the car. Thanks to our AAA membership, help arrived in an hour and we were towed into the nearest town.

Friday at nine o'clock in the evening is not the most propitious time to arrive in a strange town seeking rescue. Paul and Tony, the tow guys who hauled us into the nearby town of Tracey, recommended the West Valley Transmission Shop. Usually the owner works on Saturday, they said. Just leave the key in the box in front with a note; then call him in the morning.

You don't have a lot of options when you are a stranger in a strange land. So we did what we were told, although not without some misgivings. Then we called my sister, who lives in Sacramento, and she picked us up about half past ten.

By eight o'clock the next morning I was on the phone. I

was still calling late in the morning when we left for Tracey, hoping to find out something. What we found was a closed shop. The helpful next door shop owner phoned the security company, then the police, and finally he located Willie Selgado in Sacramento, where he had been attending a seminar. Within an hour he was back in Tracey and had secured both the car and the trailer, promising he would get on the job first thing in the morning so we could be on our way.

I didn't tell you that I called Oregon to talk to our adopted son Jeff, the family's mechanical genius. He warned me what we could be in for. It wouldn't surprise him if the tow truck operators and the shop owner were in cahoots, he said. We agreed that the problem sounded like nothing worse than a bad seal, but we both knew the mechanic could recommend a rebuilt transmission. Paul, as he was towing us in, mentioned something about $4,000 for a transmission. I gulped and prepared for the worst.

When I reached Willie by phone at half past eight Sunday morning, he told us he had the car running and was just waiting for me to show up with the trailer key so he could hook it up and give the car a test drive. We were there by ten o'clock, did the test, and I steeled myself as he asked me to sign the bill.

Quickly scanning the page, I couldn't find the price. What I found instead was a list of parts (bolts, quart-and-a-half of transmission fluid, etc.), a recommendation to have a trans-cooler installed, and a wish for a happy and safe journey. He charged me nothing—nothing for cutting short his time in Sacramento, nothing for coming in early on Sunday morning before church, nothing for the labor or the parts. When I tried to make it right, he refused. It wouldn't be right, he said. It's Sunday. Besides, he had been stranded himself in the past and knew what it felt like.

As we drove away I couldn't help thinking of Philippians 4:19, *My God will meet all your needs according to his glorious riches in Christ Jesus.* Unable to rescue myself (I really should never take to the highway without a personal attending mechanic along!), we were rescued from my ability-poverty by a stranger who could have taken advantage of our helplessness, but instead supplied our every need. I'll never forget Willie Selgado, agent of God!

A little reflection led to a day of thanksgiving. How many times, and in how many ways, has the Lord supplied my needs—according to *His* riches! How often have I been confronted with situations in which my very limited or non-existent abilities required a rescue operation, which the Lord performed. How many agents of God have I known? Too many to enumerate, too often to take for granted.

What God's promise means

As I said, it probably seems like a precariously thin thread that connects my "breakdown on the highway" story to Boaz's rescue of Ruth and Naomi. What holds the two events together is the conviction that in great things and small Paul's affirmation holds true: God *does* supply our needs, and when we are crippled by our poverty (material or otherwise) He brings His riches to our rescue.

I am stating this as carefully as I can. God supplies our needs, not our *wants*. I know, I know. Preachers of the prosperity gospel will always add, "But Jesus said, *'Ask and it will be given to you; seek and you will find; knock and the door will be opened to you. For everyone who asks receives; he who seeks finds; and to him who knocks, the door will be opened'*" (Matthew 7:7, 8). Jesus wants us rich, they insist. He owns the cattle on a thousand hills, and He wants us to have a bunch of them. It is inexcusable to be a Christian and be poor.

I thought of this shallow, unrealistic, and even heretical teaching on a recent trip to India. Everywhere you look the people's deprivation assaults your sensibilities. Christians aren't exempt, either. Are they poor because they haven't asked for more? Because they don't have faith? Because they have offended God? What exactly is the "it" that Jesus promises? If it is wealth, why aren't more Christians rich? For that matter, if it is wealth, why wasn't Jesus rich?

"The world has been enriched more by the poverty of its saints than by the wealth of its millionaires," someone has said. Jesus Himself was so poor He confessed He had no place to lay His head, yet who has enriched the world more than He? The "it" must be something other, something undoubtedly better, than mere material prosperity.

David Reagan's story of his discovery of that "something better" will be helpful to us here. David wasn't always a preacher; as a younger adult he was a businessman, a less-than-successful businessman, I should add. One evening he was in the store of his failed business, making phone calls to find a buyer for his fixtures, when he heard a knock at the front door. Irritated, he looked through the window and saw a Vietnamese man and his wife. Reagan pointed to the sign he had placed on the door that read: "CLOSED: Going Out of Business." The man knocked again. Reagan was in no mood for company. "Can't you read? We're closed!" Then the man said he was interested in buying the store's fixtures.

At that Reagan happily let them in. After they looked the store over, the Vietnamese man thanked him but explained he was opening up a different type of store. These fixtures wouldn't do.

As the couple stepped through the door to leave, the man turned back, "I discern that you are troubled in the spirit. Do you want to talk about it?"

No, he didn't, especially to a stranger. He was trapped, though. The lady went on, but Reagan and his visitor stepped into the office and the man began to talk. He narrated how, when he was a small boy, his father came home terrified. "The Communists are coming," he said, "and they are going to kill us because we are devout Catholics."

He instructed everyone in the house to get two pillow slips and go into the living room. He then ran all over the house gathering up the things he wanted to keep. "Put these in the pillow slips," he said, "and tie the tops."

Then their wealthy family escaped with only what the pillowcases could hold. They wandered in the jungle for three weeks, all twelve of them, crying out to God to save them. He did. They made it from Hanoi to safety in Saigon.

After many years he himself came home one day to tell his family and aged parents, "Get the pillow slips. The Communists are coming again." Because of his work as a translator at the American Embassy, his life was in mortal danger. The Embassy could not arrange for all his family, and he wouldn't leave without them, so once again the whole family had to run.

This time they fled to the Mekong Delta, and again they cried to God for deliverance. They wandered for several days, making it to the South China Sea where they joined a boat full of refugees about to depart. This was their second deliverance.

But once at sea, the overcrowded boat began to sink. Some panicked and began to push others overboard. Some even threw their children into the sea. The man and his family got on their knees and called to God. Then a merchant ship appeared and took the survivors on board. God saved them a third time.

They were taken with other refugees to a concentration-type camp in the Philippines. There they prayed for a new home, and a year later the news came that they were being adopted by a Bible church in Dallas, Texas. A fourth deliverance.

"So, here we are in a new land starting our lives over. God is so good. He loves us, and He answers our prayers. Lean on Him. He will deliver you."

When he left the store, David Reagan said everything had changed—yet nothing visible had changed. Gone were the self-pity and despair and in their place he had hope. "I knew in my soul that God had heard my prayer and that He had sent that man to assure me that if I would trust in the Lord, everything would turn out all right."[1]

The critical point of Dr. Reagan's story is twofold: trust

in the Lord—and let the Lord define the "it." The Reagans are still not wealthy, but their every need *has* been met. Through the Vietnamese man God was already at work rescuing David; as a young Mexican-American mechanic came to the rescue of our stranded family; as Boaz became God's instrument in delivering Ruth and Naomi from their poverty.

According to His riches

The emphasis in these stories, and most certainly in the Biblical account of Ruth, is far removed from the classic American adage, "Pick yourself up by your own bootstraps." Naomi and Ruth simply could not have made it on their own. I am not denying Naomi the praise she is due for her initiative, nor Ruth for her beauty of body and character. The stark truth is, however, that financially speaking they had nothing and Boaz had everything. Without his generosity the story would have a very different ending.

Boaz is not their crucial benefactor, however. He acknowledges a higher source of providence. *"May the Lord repay you for what you have done,"* he says to Ruth. *"May you be richly rewarded by the Lord, the God of Israel, under whose wings you have come to take refuge"* (2:12).

When we turn from this Old Testament passage to the teachings of Jesus, we find Christ returning again and again to the theme of God's providential care, His readiness to liberate us from every threat and danger. Consider Jesus' portrait of God. He is like

• a shepherd who leaves most of his flock safely in the fold to search for one lost lamb;

• a woman who turns a house upside down looking for a lost coin;

• a father searching the horizon in the hope of seeing his prodigal son coming home;

• a wealthy king who hosts a banquet for the least worthy persons in his kingdom;

- a physician who actually looks for sick people to heal (without requiring an appointment or demanding prepayment);
- a lowly Samaritan who rescues a bludgeoned victim that the religiously righteous deliberately ignored.

Scripture presents Jesus Himself as a holy man who is not uncomfortable in the company of social reprobates; a friend who openly embraces the very ones who denied, betrayed, and deserted Him; and a Savior who rescues us in our weakness and poverty. "I will be your strength, your wealth," He promises. *"Come to me, all you who are weary and burdened, and I will give you rest"* (Matthew 11:28). Our hope is in His riches.

I mentioned the trip to India. It was our third. Even though we had been to the subcontinent before, there was as always something intimidating about traveling in the interior. On our first visit we were obviously apprehensive. We couldn't read the signs, we didn't understand the culture, we felt pressed on every side by the teeming masses. If we had been left to ourselves, we would have panicked.

But we weren't alone, before or now. Leah Moshier, longtime American missionary who has devoted more than fifty years to caring for India's unwanted children, once again made certain that we were met at the airport and taken by hand every step of the way to the mission village. We relaxed, unafraid. We had no Indian money; she paid for everything. We didn't know the way; she was the way. We had only to trust; she provided everything. Had we relied only on our own resources, we might still be wandering the countryside, unable to read the signs, unable to speak the language, unable to get work. As it was, we had only to ask, seek, knock . . .

It is in this sense, I believe, and not in the selfish grasping, "Lord, give me the prosperity I seek and deserve," that Jesus encourages us to seek His hand.

According to His <u>people</u>

The human hero of Ruth's story is Boaz, the generous kinsman, the thoroughly good man who comes to the rescue. The human hero of David Reagan's story is a humble Vietnamese businessman. The human hero of our automobile-breakdown story is a bighearted Mexican-American mechanic. The human hero of our Indian visit is an experienced, generous woman missionary.

The *human* heroes.

But you and I know the real source of the rescues, don't we?

---

[1] Reagan, David R. *Trusting God*. Shreveport, LA: Huntington House, Inc., 1987.

GEAR UP

1. What kinds of poverty have you experienced?

2. Whom did God send to be your rescuer?

3. Did you recognize His hand in your rescue at the time? Explain your answer.

4. What are some of the "its" God has defined for you?

5. How can focusing on the grace acrostic (**G**od's **R**iches **A**t **C**hrist's **E**xpense) direct our thoughts away from the prosperity gospel and back to the true riches God has promised us?

6. Dr. Lawson asks us to consider Jesus' portrait of God (page 40). Which portrait touches you most deeply? Why?

7. Take a moment right now and think about other portraits of God as our rescuer that are revealed in Jesus in the Gospels. Again, which of these images touch you most deeply? Why?

8. When Dr. Lawson tells how Leah Moshier became the way for him and his wife when they were in India, he gives us insight about Jesus being "the way." If we are able to relax when we are in the hands of another human, what reasons would there be for us not to be at peace at all times in the hands of Jesus?

9. How has knowing God as your rescuer enabled you to reach out to others?

10. What character qualities do you need to develop in order to be interested in, and willing to, lead others to the Rescuer?

4
RESCUED FROM
UNBELIEVERS
1 Kings 18:17-40

THERE IS SOMETHING very modern about Elijah's contest with the prophets of Baal. The language of the Old Testament is strange to us, admittedly, steeped as it is in an ancient religious culture whose ways are not our ways. But the issue is spiritual warfare, a topic as contemporary as today's Christian best-sellers. Who is in charge here, anyway, God or the adversary? Who can be trusted, the prophet of the most high God or the priests of the opposition?

In Elijah's day and in ours, Paul's description of spiritual warfare rings true: *For though we live in the world, we do not wage war as the world does* (2 Corinthians 10:3). There is something very otherworldly about Elijah's struggle with Baal's prophets, something reminiscent of one of Paul's warnings: *For our struggle is not against flesh and blood, but against the rulers, against the authorities, against the powers of this dark world and against the spiritual forces of evil in the heavenly realms* (Ephesians 6:12). More is involved here than the incantations of frenzied priests bathed in the aroma of roast beef. The choice between Baal and God is a choice between spiritual realities, all right, but more vitally, it's between ultimate good and pervasive evil.

Today's preacher can't help identifying with Elijah. The priests of Baal are so many and so seeming-powerful. At least that's how I sometimes felt in the early days of my ministry. I seemed so puny, so powerless, so poor, so lacking in credibility, especially when I left my humble little flock in our humble little building for the halls of academe where the intelligentsia inveighed against religion in general and Christianity in particular. In 1999 Minnesota's wrestling Governor Ventura made the headlines with his *Playboy* interview condemning all religious people as weak-minded. He only brought to general attention what every university student on most secular campuses hears all the time. The battle for minds and souls today is no less intense than Elijah's spiritual tug-of-war with the priests.

Another element in the story has a pretty modern ring to it, also. The issue must be settled *scientifically.* *"If the Lord is God, follow him; but if Baal is God, follow him,"* Elijah challenges the people. "And you don't have to take my word for it. Let's run an experiment here. I'll prove who the true God is. Here's the deal. Let *the four hundred and fifty prophets of Baal and the four hundred prophets of Asherah, who eat at Jezebel's table* prepare two bulls for sacrifice on an altar, and I will do the same. *Then you call on the name of your god, and I will call on the name of the Lord. The god who answers by fire—he is God."*

The scientific test—two altars, two bulls. The test sample, the control group. A simple demonstration of power under closely controlled conditions.

Elijah is convinced that only the true God can pull it off.

The prophet's prayer is simple: *"Answer me, O Lord, answer me, so these people will know that you, O Lord, are God, and that you are turning their hearts back again."*

After the pleading and wailing of the false prophets (or, more accurately, the prophets of the false god), Elijah's simple supplication needs no histrionics. "Just let the people know the truth, Lord, just let them know, so they will come back home to You." Unspoken is his desire that they not be impressed with the numbers of the many priests but rather with the power of the one God.

King Henry V, in Shakespeare's play by that name, implores God before the battle of Agincourt on behalf of his troops,

> O God of battles! Steel my soldiers' hearts;
> Possess them not with fear; take from them now
> The sense of reckoning, if the opposed numbers
> Pluck their hearts from them!

If battles were determined by numbers of combatants alone, Henry's Englishmen would die at the hands of the French. If mere "reckoning," adding up the "opposed numbers" were the deciding factor, the English were doomed. So was Elijah. So, it must be said, are we.

What conclusions can we draw from this spectacular contest on Mount Carmel? There are several, and they are enough.

The victory does not always go to the majority.

Perhaps this is the biggest lesson to be learned here. At least it is the one that has taken me the better part of a lifetime to learn. The majority is not always right. The voice of the people is *not* the voice of God.

As a citizen, I had to learn that the rule of the majority is not by a long shot the rule of the righteous. Although at times in my ministry I have felt a little like Elijah *(I am the only one of the Lord's prophets left, but Baal has four hundred and fifty prophets),* with the passing of time I have increasingly been able to take comfort in this truth. I have learned that if the majority is for something, it is probably not the best idea!

As a person, I had to learn that just because something is legal it is not necessarily moral (even though a *majority* enacted the law and believe that "legal equals moral").

As a Christian, I had to learn that the church is not a democracy; therefore spiritual issues cannot justly be decided by asking, "What do the members want?"

48 Rescued!

A popular-poll-governed democracy causes me to fear for the future. In the battle of spiritual forces, how can we trust leaders who care more about being reelected than about doing what's right for their constituency?

People my age and older can remember Florida's Governor Fuller Warren, who in the fifties was a master at reading his constituents and telling them what they wanted to hear. He was running for office in a year that counties were voting their local option on permitting the sale of liquor. As one who used to live in a dry county in Tennessee, I can testify that passions ran high between the "wets" and the "dries" in those days. (One of my political friends assured me that whenever the issue was up for a vote in our county, the preachers and their allies, the bootleggers, campaigned to keep the county dry.) Warren's stance on the issue was classic.

"*If by whisky*, you mean the water of life that cheers men's souls, that smoothes out the tensions of the day, that gives gentle perspective to one's view of life, then put my name on the list of the fervent wets.

"*If by whisky,* you mean the devil's brew that rends families, destroys careers, and ruins one's ability to work, then count me in the ranks of the dries."

The voice of the people!

Warren's slipperiness needs to be balanced by the account of another politician, Harry Truman. I was a teenager when he left office. One of the surprises of these recent years is that the man about whom I heard nothing good in his second term (when I was just becoming conscious of politicians) is now considered one of our strongest and, according to an increasing number of historians, one of our best presidents. When Truman amazed the nation with his upset victory over Thomas Dewey in 1948, General George Marshall told him he had "put over the greatest one-man fight in American history. You did exactly what you told me and what nobody else believed possible."

Clark Clifford commented on this victory in later years.

While conceding that Truman was a skilled, sensible politician, he insisted that Truman won the presidency because of his remarkable courage, "his refusal to be discouraged, his willingness to go through the suffering of that campaign, the fatigue, the will to fight every step of the way, the will to win . . . "[1]

Truman's story resonates with the David and Goliath story, doesn't it? And with Elijah's confrontation with the priests of Baal. We like to see the little guy win. Not only do we want the underdog to come out on top, but we want truth and righteousness to win as well. We have learned that the majority isn't always right and the big guys aren't always righteous.

The victory does not always go to the ritualists (dancing).

Then they called on the name of Baal from morning till noon. "O Baal, answer us!" they shouted. But there was no response; no one answered. And they danced around the altar they had made.

All religions have their rituals. These stylized ceremonies are supposed to open the door to God, to cause Him to look with favor upon the supplicants and to grant their wishes. Whenever religion is attacked, this formalized behavior is ridiculed—but never eliminated. Believers hold experts in the performance of ritual in highest esteem. They seem to be so much closer to God than the rest of us.

It's an understandable practice. No matter how proficient we are in our native language, something more seems needed, something somehow more "holy." So some believers adopt a "prayer language" that rises above the common tongue, and eccentric body movements (eccentric only to the outsider) that symbolize a special relationship between themselves and their God. After all, the divine can't be approached as we approach one another (although we shouldn't overlook the mating dance, I suppose).

The four hundred fifty priests of Baal are supreme ritualists. They are good at their job. But thank God, God is not impressed. The prophet Amos, quoting the Lord, makes this abundantly clear: *"I hate, I despise your religious feasts; I cannot stand your assemblies. Even though you bring me burnt offerings and grain offerings, I will not accept them. Though you bring choice fellowship offerings, I will have no regard for them. Away with the noise of your songs! I will not listen to the music of your harps. But let justice roll on like a river, righteousness like a never-failing stream!"* (Amos 5:21-24).

So much for the power of rituals, then.

The victory does not always go to the loudest.

At noon Elijah began to taunt them. "Shout louder!" he said. "Surely he is a god! Perhaps he is deep in thought, or busy, or traveling. Maybe he is sleeping and must be awakened." So they shouted louder . . .

The priests can't wake up Baal, but they don't fail for lack of trying. And not for lack of volume. (Could we read this passage as a cautionary tale for contemporary musicians, who often seem to measure their effectiveness in decibels? Do they think they can impress the gods with amplifiers that insure the wholesale deafness of the audience? Just wondering.)

While the priests are yelling we are recalling Jesus. *"Be careful not to do your 'acts of righteousness' before men, to be seen by them. If you do, you will have no reward from your Father in heaven. So when you give to the needy, do not announce it with trumpets, as the hypocrites do in the synagogues and on the streets, to be honored by men. I tell you the truth, they have received their reward in full"* (Matthew 6:1, 2).

They want to be heard by men. They are heard by men. Period. There's no evidence they are heard by God. Neither, it appears, are the prophets of Baal.

The victory does not always go to the multiplying of pray-ers.

This is perhaps the most sobering aspect of the Mount Carmel contest. The odds are 850 to 1, and the 1 is the victor. It takes only one pray-er, if his or her prayer is to the one God. Again we are reminded of Jesus' instruction on prayer: *"And when you pray, do not be like the hypocrites, for they love to pray standing in the synagogues and on the street corners to be seen by men. I tell you the truth, they have received their reward in full. But when you pray, go into your room, close the door and pray to your Father, who is unseen. Then your Father, who sees what is done in secret, will reward you. And when you pray, do not keep on babbling like pagans, for they think they will be heard because of their many words. Do not be like them, for your Father knows what you need before you ask him"* (Matthew 6:5-8).

What should we think, then, when earnest souls beg us to join them in praying for a worthy cause: someone's healing, the return of the country to Christian values, the successful conclusion of a building fund campaign, peace in our time, or whatever? "We want to get everybody praying," they tell us. There's power in numbers.

Yet Jesus teaches the opposite. We aren't heard for our many words, or our amassing of numbers of prayers. *Go into your room, close the door and pray to your Father who is unseen. Then your Father, who sees what is done in secret, will reward you.*

I am asking for trouble here, I know. We have become so accustomed to orchestrated prayer campaigns that my interpretation of Elijah's experience seems little short of heretical. I am probably guilty of reading my biases into the Scripture. True, the Mount Carmel contest isn't about the rules of prayer. But I can't help wondering, in light of it, whether there is any scriptural justification for thinking a prayer is more powerful because many are praying it? Just a question.

The Mount Carmel contest isn't over how many are

praying, but about how great is the God to whom they are praying.

The victory does not always go to the self-flagellating,

So they shouted louder and slashed themselves with swords and spears, as was their custom, until their blood flowed.

Little needs to be added here. Even though certain holy men and certain sects and cults call attention to their religiosity by every kind of masochistic behavior, this is one heresy comfort-loving Americans for the most part have managed to avoid. With the exception of radical fringe groups, we aren't into mutilating ourselves to appease the gods.

nor to the officially religious,

The priests of Baal and Asherah are privileged men. They are the court's religious. They enjoy the favor of the king and queen and, supposedly, of their god.

What sobers this officially ordained minister when reading this passage (and so many others like it) is that in the Bible it's usually the officially righteous persons who are the bad guys. Jesus is pretty tender to the outsider, the downtrodden, and the self-acknowledged sinner; He saves His anger for the self-righteous, self-proclaimed officials of religion.

Clergymen, beware.

nor to the popular.

It's fair to say that the "troubler of Israel" is not exactly a hit with the king and his court. The general population does not hurry to stand with him in his contest, either. Genuine prophets (truth-tellers) are seldom invited to a party. Party-goers, like political party-liners, are not all that committed to the truth, especially when it's not popular.

To the extent that Christians are truth-tellers to a nation worshiping false gods, we have to expect rejection. Some of our unpopularity we deserve. When we claim to be the *moral* majority, implying that everyone else is *immoral*, we invite ridicule. They can see through us, these *immoral* ones. They read our inconsistencies, laugh at our lack of logic, point out our all-too-obvious failures. When we condemn them, how can we expect praise?

But sometimes we are stumbling blocks simply because of what we stand for. *"All men will hate you because of me,"* Jesus warned His disciples, but then added encouragingly, *"but he who stands firm to the end will be saved"* (Mark 13:13). Disciples of one who was executed on a cross for insulting the leaders of established religion cannot hope for different treatment when they take up His cause. They will lose. But the decisive victory will not necessarily belong to the well-liked.

Here's what I mean. In 1996 David Kessler stepped down as the controversial head of the Food and Drug Administration. He must have been relieved to leave his Washington post, since he had been a "troubler of Israel" throughout his tenure. Resisting the pressure, even the threats, of some of Washington's most powerful lobbies, he pursued a course demanding rigidly high standards for the new products his department tested. To be honest, I never thought I would read the tribute *US News and World Report* paid him. First this: "Whatever one thinks of his tenure, it is difficult to dispute his integrity, or the moral force of his actions." Then this: "Moral courage is rare because it requires a willingness to walk away—from prestige, from one's livelihood, in extreme cases from life itself." And finally, "In a city where too often the lesson is 'Do as I say, not as I do,' David Kessler is somebody you can tell your children about."[2]

He was never popular. Just right. But it was only after he was safely out of office that his virtue was praised. When he was on the job he was hated.

So we praise Elijah—now.

The victory does not always go to the indecisive.

The people are confronted with a simple choice: *Elijah went before the people and said, "How long will you waver between two opinions? <u>If the Lord is God, follow him</u>; but if Baal is God, follow him."*

As always in the Scripture, the choice is between kinds of service, not between independence and dependence. You will worship some god. Shouldn't it be *the* God?

But the people can't decide. They say nothing. It's no wonder the Bible calls us sheep. It has been pointed out that if you hold a stick in front of the foremost sheep in the flock that files down a trail in the mountains, he will jump it and every sheep following will jump when he reaches the spot, even if the stick is removed. So the people on Mount Carmel. They remind us of Matthew Arnold's awful choice in "A Summer Night."

> Is there no life, but these alone?
> Madman or slave, must man be one?

To a people accustomed to slavery, taking a stand against the majority seems madness.

No one ever said following the Lord would be easy. But it beats bondage, don't you think?

You probably know the famous legend from India about the mouse that was terrified of cats. A magician, pitying the pathetic coward, agreed to transform him into a cat. That worked splendidly, until it met a dog. Then the magician turned the cowering cat into a dog. All went well until it met a tiger. So the magician turned him into a tiger, thus taming his fears. But when the tiger came back complaining that he had met a hunter, the magician refused to help. "I will make you into a mouse again, for though you have the body of a tiger, you still have the heart of a mouse."

Mouse-hearts are in unlimited supply.

The victory goes to God.

The victory belongs to God, from whom all courage flows. In this case as in the others we are studying, what is required of the believer is not extraordinary strength or superior spirituality or poll-winning popularity or anything other than this: to have the courage to stand alone, against the majority if necessary, on behalf of your God. Then God Himself rescues you—according to His purposes.

Which is what happened to Elijah.

---

[1]McCullough, David. *Truman.* New York, et al: Simon and Schuster, 1992.

[2]Goode, Erica E., "Real-Life Courage." *US News and World Report* 121 (12/9/96): 11

GEAR UP

1. Whether we realize it or not, Christians are engaged in spiritual warfare. Reread the Scriptures on page 45. Who is our enemy in this battle? Describe his forces.

2. Consider the enemy's strategy in 2 Corinthians 11:14, 15 and Revelation 12:10, 11. How does he attract us?

3. Were you involved in such a battle recently? What happened?

4. Elijah prayed on behalf of others and so can we. Who are some of the people you pray for regularly?

5. What has happened in their lives as a result of your prayers?

6. What are some words that describe how you feel when you hear politicians double-talking, trying to get your vote?

7. What are some words that describe how you feel when "the little guy" wins?

8. When have you had to stand alone for God?

9. How did you feel when you were in the middle of it?

58 *Rescued!*

10. In what ways were you able to appropriate God's power?

11. What are some things that you wish you had done differently?

5
RESCUED FROM
THE IMPOSSIBLE

2 Kings 6:8-23

THE YOUNG MAN in my office was considering whether to accept a job offer. He was obviously intrigued, challenged even, but uncertain whether it was for him. He wasn't sure he could do it. It seemed too big, almost impossible. "What should I do?" he wanted to know.

I answered by recounting my own career for him. I was forty years old before moving to take up a new job that I thought I could do. That was a first for me. Every other "real" position I had held, beginning as a nineteen-year-old church youth director through my years as a college vice-president and senior minister, had me gasping for air while learning to swim on the job. At forty we moved to Arizona where I was to be the senior minister of a church only a little over half the size of the one I was serving in Indiana. This one, I thought, I can handle. Then the church quickly outgrew anything my previous experience had prepared me for, so I was once again swimming in water over my head.

Throughout my working career God has had to rescue me from impossible situations. And here I am now, in my sixties, trying to help a little Bible college grow into a university. The impossibles seem to be ganging up on me again—challenges from the accrediting association, from skeptical constituents, from enemies determined to bring us down. (Before sitting down to write this chapter today, my assistant called with the bad news of yet another frivolous lawsuit.) And ahead lies the challenge of merging our institution with two other struggling schools. As I write these words I confess that, humanly speaking, I am uncertain whether we'll succeed. We don't have the resources, if everything is up to us.

But is it all up to us? And what if it all looked doable? What if we had "all our ducks in a row"? What if we had the money in hand to do everything we wanted to do? Where would be the challenge? The sense of accomplishment? The reliance on God?

On the other hand, what if we fail? What if in fact we've misread God's signals and this is not what He has in mind at all, not at all?

Do I sound as if I've spent some long nights on these questions? I have. But I'll tell you something that would be worse than having to overcome the obstacles I see ahead, worse than wondering how we'll find the strength, gain the insight, marshal the resources to meet these challenges. Far worse would be finding ourselves chained to the merely possible. To undertake only if success is guaranteed. To be limited to our own abilities.

So my counsel to the young man was to take the job *because* he wasn't sure he could handle it. Otherwise he would never know the extent of his own abilities. And certainly he would not have the exhilarating experience of being rescued from his insufficiency by God's all-sufficiency. He could never say, *I can do all things <u>through Christ</u> which strengtheneth me* (Philippians 4:13, KJV), nor could he comprehend the marvelous paradox, *For when I am weak, then I am strong* (2 Corinthians 12:10).

I encouraged him, in other words, to try walking by faith. The world has no shortage of cautious souls who have scared themselves into safe, secure routines that will never reveal their potential and never expose the resources of God waiting to be summoned to their aid. They may have read John's promise in 1 John 4:4 that *the one who is in you is greater than the one who is in the world,* but you couldn't prove it by their actions. What they can't see, can't touch, or can't control, they can't believe in.

They are like Elisha's servant, nearly paralyzed by fright when he sees the hostile Arameans surrounding the city. To him the situation is hopeless, impossible. *"Oh, my lord, what shall we do?"* He can't think of a thing. Everywhere he looks he sees the hostile forces of Aram ready to charge the city. There are too many of *them*, too few of *us*. The situation is impossible.

Elisha, seeing deeper than his servant, calms him. *"Don't be afraid . . . those who are with us are more than those who are with them."*

We have unseen resources.

Elisha's words should be engraved on every believer's heart. His are not the comforting words of my grandmother, "There, there. Everything's going to be all right." No, sometimes everything *isn't* going to be all right. This is still an "us against them" world. Everything wasn't all right when Elijah stood up to the priests of untruth. Everything wasn't all right for Naomi and her daughters-in-law. Certainly things weren't all right in Noah's world, or Gideon's. But what Elisha, the man of God, knows that his servant doesn't is that there is more to this world than meets the eye. True, the city of Dothan is surrounded by Arameans. But the man of God is surrounded by God's horses and chariots of fire.

It's just that the servant can't see them.

What separates the prophet from his servant is his eyesight. Only Elisha has eyes to see what lies beyond the range of his servant's myopia. Jonathan Swift defined vision as "the art of seeing things invisible." Such is Elisha's vision. What a difference this "second sight" makes. As Frederick Langbridge has written,

> Two men look out through the same bars:
> One sees the mud, and one the stars.

62 Rescued!

Elisha can see the stars. He quells his despairing servant's panic by asking the Lord to show him what the prophet can see. *Then the Lord opened the servant's eyes, and he looked and saw the hills full of horses and chariots of fire all around Elisha.*

Whenever I read this passage I can't help wondering, "But what if the servant refuses to see? What if he is certain his spiritual short-sightedness can see all there is to see? What if he concludes that his master has, at long last, taken leave of his senses, that his much praying has led him to delusions? The questions are not as far-fetched as they may seem. Any experienced Christian leader, granted a vision of such a future, has had his dreams punctured by the naysayer, the contrarian who could not see, because he would not.

These willfully blind obstructionists came to mind as I read Oliver Sacks' account of Greg, a blind patient whose amnesia Dr. Sacks was attempting to treat. Greg could remember songs from 1964 to 1968, but his memory cut off around 1970 or earlier. Sacks calls him "a fossil, the last hippie." He was stuck in the era of the flower children. Upon examination, the doctor found Greg's eyes showed complete optic atrophy. It was physically impossible for him to see anything. Yet Greg was not aware he was blind. He readily admitted his eyes "weren't all that good," but said he enjoyed watching the TV. That exercise consisted of following the soundtrack of a movie or show and inventing the visual scenes to go with it. He was blind to his blindness.

Dr. Sacks came to realize that Greg had actually lost any understanding as to what seeing or looking meant. His loss "seemed to point to something stranger, and more complex, than a mere 'deficit,' to point, rather, to some radical alteration within him in the very structure of knowledge, in consciousness, in identity itself." This might not have been so scary except that Greg was convinced he was completely normal. When the doctors tried to give him an opportunity to learn Braille, he balked. "What's going on? Do you think I'm blind? Why am I here, with blind people all around me?

... If I were blind, I would be the first person to know it."[1] But he was the last to know. He would never know. He had lost his potential for change. He could not see because he would not.

His number is legion. I have met people like Greg on church boards, on college campuses, in every walk of life. Haven't you? Surrounded by the resources God lavishes on us, these Gregs are vision-impaired. They will not see, therefore they will not make use of God's available assets. They are trapped in Dothan.

We have the power of prayer.

In the previous chapter I raised questions about the rather puzzling confidence we place in praying by numbers: The more people praying, the greater the assurance we have that we will get what we pray for. It didn't work that way in Elijah's case. And in Elisha's the lesson is the same. One man prays boldly, and God delivers.

The power is not in the praying but in the God who hears the prayers.

And Elisha prayed, "O Lord, open his eyes so he may see." Then the Lord opened the servant's eyes, and he looked and saw the hills full of horses and chariots of fire all around Elisha. As the enemy came down toward him, Elisha prayed to the Lord, "Strike these people with blindness." So he struck them with blindness, as Elisha had asked.

I also wrote earlier about Harry Truman. When Franklin Delano Roosevelt died suddenly on April 12, 1945, this most surprising of American presidents was catapulted into office. Many historians have commented on Truman's lack of preparation for the job, and on Roosevelt's astonishing denial of his declining health and his refusal to prepare his successor. The untried Truman was just trying out the seat behind the president's desk for the first time when Admiral William Leahy, Roosevelt's personal chief of staff and now his, laid a stack of urgent papers before him. The trial had

64 *Rescued!*

begun. Later that day the overwhelmed chief executive told reporters, "Boys, if you ever pray, pray for me now. I don't know whether you fellows ever had a load of hay fall on you, but when they told me yesterday what happened, I felt like the moon, the stars, and all the planets had fallen on me." He later admitted to his friend, Senator George Aiken, "I'm not big enough for this job." But he was. He was willing to tap resources beyond his own abilities.

Instructive, isn't it, this intuitive reference to praying, this assumption that the greater the challenge the greater the need for divine assistance? Little things like the vice-presidency Truman could handle on his own, but the presidency? Pray, boys, pray.

I like this prayer someone sent to me:
> Dear Lord,
> so far today, God, I've done all right.
> I haven't lost my temper,
> Haven't been greedy, grumpy, nasty,
> Selfish, or over-indulgent.
> I'm really glad about that,
> But, in a few minutes,
> God, I am going to get out of bed,
> And from then on
> I'm probably going to need
> A lot more help.
> Thank You, in Jesus' name.
> Amen.

What I like about this whimsical prayer is not just the humor, but the reality it addresses. In big things (like suddenly becoming president) *and* little (like facing a new day), we need help. The battle for righteousness is fought not only in extreme crises but in the little vexations of everyday living. Paul's counsel to pray constantly (1 Thessalonians 5:17) implies God's ready helpfulness in all circumstances. We *feel* the need more when the crisis hits ("Pray, boys, pray") but *have* the need even when we don't feel it.

We can see the unseen that is really there.

Elisha's experience may strike you as more than passing strange. His vision reveals *the hills full of horses and chariots of fire.* Moderns readily dismiss the account. Mere superstition, they insist, this belief in a populated, unseen world.

We children of the Enlightenment pride ourselves in how far we've come from the Dark Ages, when the invisible world teemed with angels, seraphim, demons, spirits, principalities, and powers. Ugly gargoyles strategically placed along the eaves protected the great cathedrals, frightened away the evil spirits. Incense was burned, incantations were intoned, whatever it took to keep the demons at bay.

We know better now, of course. Our scientists scoff at such primitive beliefs—while they carry on rather smugly about quarks, quasars, electrons and protons and neutrons, and other fanciful critters no one has ever seen but the existence of which these physicists testify with undoubting faith. They believe in a richly populated unseen universe, this one of their own creating.

I am unprepared to do battle with them. Their inventions may in fact describe invisible reality. All I am suggesting is that whatever language describes it (scriptural or mythological or scientific), the world's biggest thinkers do agree that there is more to reality than meets the eye. Since this is so, we would be well advised not to be too hasty in rejecting what we have not personally experienced. Bran Ferren (former president of Walt Disney Imagineering, now co-chairman of Applied Minds), reminds us that people in theater never anticipated film, and film people never anticipated television, and television people never anticipated cable, and cable people never anticipated the Internet and. . . . Who knows what else is out there?

So Elisha, on intimate terms with God, can see what his servant misses. I suspect this is the natural result of walking with the Lord, don't you? He enables us to see farther and deeper into things. He brings comfort in the face of terror (*Yea, though I walk through the valley of the shadow of death,*

I will fear no evil: for thou art with me, Psalm 23:4, KJV).

I'm impressed with people in the secular realm who have this gift of far-seeing.

Thomas Jefferson offers a good example. When as president he dispatched Lewis and Clark on their epic journey across the continent, he was dreaming of a nation that would stretch from shore to shore. Very few shared his vision. They couldn't imagine it would be possible to govern an area so large. Distances were too great and travel too slow. They had the facts (as they were known as the nineteenth century began) on their side. In 1801 nothing moved faster than the speed of a horse. Period. Nothing ever had, ever would, they'd assure you. The best road in the country was from Boston to New York, and even on that highway the 175 miles required three full days for a light stagecoach carrying only passengers, their baggage, and the mail, and that was by exchanging spent horses for fresh ones at every way station.

As I said, they had the facts. But Jefferson had the imagination. In another example, even before he became president he saw (1793) a hot-air balloon and wished he could appropriate one for his own travel. With it, he wrote his daughter Martha, he could be home in five hours instead of the normal ten days. How he would enjoy the jet travel of our day. I doubt he would be surprised.

Neither should we be surprised that some of God's servants belong in Elisha's company, seeing far and seeing through, and that Elisha's servant is always with us, scared, unseeing, requiring a special revelation before he can take comfort in the presence of God's rescue team.

We can experience serenity in the face of the enemy's threats.

The fast-moving narrative wastes no time with any probing of Elisha's psyche. One thing comes across, though. Elisha is a man at peace with himself and with God. He could have sung with David, *I will lie down and sleep in peace, for you alone, O Lord, make me dwell in safety* (Psalm 4:8). He has learned well the lesson Paul passes on to the Christians in Philippi: *Do not be anxious about anything, but in everything, by prayer and petition, with thanksgiving, present your requests to God. And the peace of God, which transcends all understanding, will guard your hearts and your minds in Christ Jesus* (Philippians 4:6, 7).

This peace is one of the great promises of Christ:

- *"I have told you these things, so that in me you may have peace. In this world you will have trouble. But take heart! I have overcome the world"* (John 16:33).
- *"Peace I leave with you; my peace I give you. I do not give to you as the world gives. Do not let your hearts be troubled and do not be afraid"* (John 14:27).

John Bunyan wrote *The Pilgrim's Progress* from jail, having been arrested for his fearless preaching of the gospel. Instead of cursing his fate, though, he produced one of history's greatest Christian classics. The peace that passes understanding, even in prison, was his experience, and of that peace he wrote. "So I saw in my dream that just as Christian came up with the Cross, his burden loosed from off his shoulders, and fell from off his back and began to tumble, and so continued to do, till it came to the mouth of the sepulchre, where it fell in, and I saw it no more. Then was Christian glad and lightsome, and said, with a merry heart, 'He has given me rest by His sorrow and life by His death.'"

William Faulkner, attempting to convey that same sense of vision-inspired peace in *The Sound and the Fury,* writes of the visiting Negro preacher in his "shabby alpaca coat, standing in the pulpit, one arm resting on the reading desk, his voice resonant with pathos, until men's hearts are 'speaking to one another . . . beyond the need of words. I see it, Brethren, I see it, the blasting, blinding sight! I see Calvary, with the sacred trees, the thief and the murderer and the least of these. I hear the boasting and the bragging, the weeping and the turned away face of God. . . . Then what is it I see?

I see the resurrection and the light, and the meek Jesus saying, "I died that they who believe might live again." Brethren, O brethren!'"

That's it, isn't it? The vision of the risen Lord—and the peace.

One final word

I have used vision in two ways in this chapter: first, as the ability to see what is already present but unseen by most people; and second, the ability to "envision," or "imagine" a future that has not yet materialized, but can be realized by a person of faith who grasps the resources God has made available to the believer. In no way have I suggested that "vision" is to be compared with "hallucination."

If the horses and chariots of fire were mere illusions, we would be pitying rather than admiring the hallucinating Elisha. The servant and not the prophet would receive our praise; his would be the voice of reason, the prophet's the ranting of a madman. But Elisha is the hero of the narrative because his faith-filled vision enables him to see something that is really there. The horses and chariots of fire are not mere figments of his imagination.

I am stressing this point because I have been reading a book of one man's quest to know the meaning of life. In his search he has consulted a wide range of seers, prophets, and preachers. It is entertaining to study the flights of fancy being passed off as wisdom in the interviews—entertaining, but misleading. Each session leaves me marveling at and doubting the visions, dreams, and spiritual visitations that are described—marveling, because they are beyond my experience; doubting, because they are such private affairs. I am unable to identify with the writer's enthusiasm for his newfound information. These men and women seem such uncertain guides to spiritual truth.

By contrast, in this passage Elisha gains credibility with his servant and with the reader when he prays that the servant may be granted the privilege of seeing what he sees, of experiencing the assurance that is his. It is not a private vision, but a shared one.

For many years Joy and I lived in a community dominated by a religious group that takes pride in the secret rites of its temple, the secret mysteries known only to the initiated, the special insights granted only to the insiders of this religion, the special position of the priesthood. Undoubtedly because of our residence there, we came to appreciate as never before the openness of the church of Christ. As a minister of the gospel, I don't know anything you can't find out. As a preacher of the Word, I have access to no mysteries or doctrines that are unavailable to you. As a visionary, I see nothing that you can't see as well. Whatever resources God makes available to me as His servant, He makes available to you. *In him and through faith in him we may approach God with freedom and confidence* (Ephesians 3:12). Not only can we come close to God, but we can do incredible things through Him. He is the one *who is able to do immeasurably more than all we ask or imagine, according to his power that is at work within us . . .* (Ephesians 3:20).

It is all available to us.

Jesus tells the truth: *"Everything is possible for him who believes"* (Mark 9:23).

---

[1]Sacks, Oliver. *An Anthropologist on Mars.* New York: Vintage Books. 1996.

GEAR UP

1. Have you ever been give a task that you thought was beyond your skills to perform? What happened as a result?

2. Has someone who had a clearer understanding of God and His Word ever helped you see something from God's Word that you had previously missed? How did he or she do this?

3. With whom do you most identify—Elisha or his servant? Why?

4. What do you learn from the frightened servant?

5. What do you learn from Elisha in the way he dealt with his servant's fears?

6. Are you a "constant pray-er" or a crisis pray-er? What are some of the excuses we use for not praying constantly? Do you believe that God is interested in every detail of your life?

7. Dr. Lawson writes, "The power is not in the praying but in the God who hears the prayers." What does this mean to you?

8. What statements about prayer does James make in James 5:13-16? How do these statements apply to your prayers?

72 *Rescued!*

9. What do you think God is wanting to teach you about prayer from these Scriptures and from Dr. Lawson's writing?

10. Men and women of vision always have seen the cross and the empty tomb. How do the preacher's words on page 67 compare with Paul's words in Philippians 3:10, 11?

11. How do the preacher's words compare with John's vision of the risen Christ (Revelation 1:12-16)?

12. How do the preacher's words compare with your own vision of Jesus?

6
RESCUED FROM
A FIERY FURNACE
Daniel 3:1-30

WHERE DO YOU GO when the highest authority in your land turns against you? When you are in serious trouble, not for doing wrong, but for believing right? When you've reached the court of last resort and have exhausted your appeals?

You turn to the highest authority *over* the land, to the one whose rule is not limited *to* the land. You listen respectfully to all Nebuchadnezzar's huffing and puffing, then quietly place your trust in God, whose authority extends even over fiery furnaces.

When we first learned the story of Shadrach, Meshach, and Abednego as children, our imaginations were enthralled by the drama itself, with its stench of burning flesh (the soldiers', not the victims'), the mystery of that fourth person in the furnace, and the miracle of the rescue.

With maturity our attention has shifted. Now it is riveted to the faith-charged courage of the three men who would rather die than deny their God. Such daring forces us to have a closer look at them before we consider the miracle itself.

Courage in the face of danger

"If we are thrown into the blazing furnace, the God we serve is able to save us from it, and he will rescue us from your hand, O king. But even if he does not, we want you to

know, O king, that we will not serve your gods or worship the image of gold you have set up."

Where did it come from, this almost incredible courage? Their answer to the king's demand reveals the source. Let's take a closer look.

God will rescue us, if He wants to.

"The God we serve is able to save us." It should be pointed out that this is no abstract faith, born of study and discussion but untested in real-life experience. It is a living trust, strengthened by their daily service in His name. They aren't relying on the God of Israel as opposed to the god of Babylonia, the god of this place instead of the god of that place. Their confidence is in the God whom they have been serving and will be serving in whatever place they find themselves, even in a fiery furnace.

With a faith born of experience, then, they trust. He is able. They believe *he will rescue us from your hand, O king.*

One of America's great World War II generals, Matthew B. Ridgway, commander of the 82nd Airborne, confessed to receiving a similar sense of assurance during the most critical periods of the war. "Sometimes, at night," he has said, "it was almost as if I could hear the assurance that God the Father gave to another soldier, named Joshua: *I will not fail thee, nor forsake thee."*[1] God the Father. Not the God of America over against the God of Germany, or the God of the Christians as opposed to the god of the Nazis. Not "Somebody Up There (Who) Likes Me." No, *the God whom we serve.*

This is He of whom the psalmist sang in so many familiar songs. Here, for example, are the words of Psalm 31. They could have been intoned by Shadrach, Meshach, and Abednego:

In you, O Lord, I have taken refuge; let me never be put to shame; deliver me in your righteousness.

Turn your ear to me, come quickly to my rescue; be my rock of refuge, a strong fortress to save me.

Since you are my rock and my fortress, for the sake of your name lead and guide me.

Free me from the trap that is set for me, for you are my refuge.

Into your hands I commit my spirit; redeem me, O Lord, the God of truth (Psalm 31:1-5).

So they believe, these three young men. God is able to rescue them if He wants to.

Even if He decides not to rescue us, we will not desert Him.

Their allegiance does not depend on His performance in *this* crisis. They won't switch sides if, for some reason, God chooses not to rescue them this time. Their security is in His judgment, not their wishes. This is the real core of the story. They refuse to strike a bargain with God: "We'll serve You if we get what we want." "Rescue us, O God. If You don't, we'll go over to Nebuchadnezzar's god." "Don't embarrass us here by not coming through for us, because if You do we'll forsake You."

The three men's steadfastness forces a question we'd rather not face. What are *our* "even ifs"? How far can we be pushed before we'll say, "Enough, already. I give." Can we boldly assert, "Even if *this* should happen, I will not give up God"? "Even if *that* doesn't come about as I expect, I'll still be here"?

For that matter, what are our "unlesses" or "only ifs"? "I'm only in this if. . . ." "Unless God comes through on this one, I'm outta here."

How deep run our loyalties, how firm our convictions? Can we be counted on when the heat's on?

From World War II comes a symbol of quiet determination. As Allied forces were on a search mission in Germany after the armistice, they came upon a wall on which a holocaust victim had etched,

> I believe in the sun, even when it does not shine.
> I believe in love, even when it is not shown.
> I believe in God, even when He is silent.

No "only if" for this believer.

I love the quiet testimony of an elderly woman named Mary in Binford, North Dakota. Her preacher Eric Hulstrand was preaching one Sunday morning when Mary fainted and struck her head on the end of the pew.

Someone immediately called an ambulance. Soon the paramedics strapped Mary onto a stretcher. Just before they headed out the door, Mary regained consciousness and motioned for her daughter to come hear. Pastor Hulstrand says everyone thought she was summoning the strength to utter what could be her final words. Her daughter bent over, her ear at her mother's mouth to hear her mother's whispered words. "My offering is in my purse."

"Even if He should slay me," as Job might have said, "He shall have my offering."

Steadfastness.

We are in this thing together!

It isn't explicitly stated in the text, but we aren't doing it an injustice to point out that Shadrach, Meshach, and Abednego are not alone in the furnace. Leaving aside the Divine Comforter for the moment, we can see that they enjoy another source of comfort. They have each other. The Bible teems with stories of great heroes who performed their heroics alone (Daniel and the lions' den comes to mind), but the truth is that most of us are not cut out of such stern stuff. We need other people to prop us up. Jesus, recognizing this truth of human nature, founded a church for just such a purpose. He knew it matters who we hang out with!

In an earlier chapter I quoted part of the famous challenge to the troops that Shakespeare put in the mouth of his Henry

V at the historic battle of Agincourt. Henry would meld his assembly of individuals into a community, a fellowship—or as he says, a band of brothers.

> From this day to the ending of the world,
> . . . we in it shall be remembered—
> . . . we band of brothers;
> For he today that sheds his blood with me
> Shall be my brother.

There's strength in numbers.

There's also duty in numbers. The three men owe it to each other to stand firm. One man's weakness can topple another. One man's resolve can strengthen the whole.

Most American schoolchildren study Lincoln's masterful Gettysburg Address as an example of the best kind of public oratory and as a fine specimen of presidential leadership. What most of us were not told in school was what a wrenching experience it was for the president to travel to Gettysburg for the event. He arrived the day before the ceremonies in time to attend a large dinner that evening. Edward Everett, who was to deliver the major address the next day, was there, his numerous admirers swarming around him. President Lincoln seemed virtually alone, a besieged commander in chief whose war was not going well. He excused himself from the after-dinner conversations to return to his room and work a bit more on his remarks. He was troubled by the war. He was also in trouble with his wife, whose telegram arrived around midnight: "The doctor has just left. We hope dear Taddie is slightly better."

Their ten-year-old was ill. Abraham and Mary already had lost two of their four children. With Tad's prognosis uncertain, she insisted he must not go to Gettysburg. He went anyway. Gettysburg was not just about the soldiers who fought there. It was his battle as much as theirs. The dead had been sacrificed for his nation's freedom. His troops would feel deserted if he stayed home. Lincoln felt as keenly as Shakespeare's Henry V that "he today that sheds his blood with me / Shall be my brother." President and foot soldier were in this thing together.

So Shadrach, Meshach, and Abednego were in their predicament together, and as a unit they went to their blazing furnace. According to the narrator, not only is there strength in numbers but their numbers are further strengthened once they get there. A fourth person appears among them. Christians have traditionally assumed, though the text does not explicitly say so, that the fourth is Christ, their Comforter and Protector. James Dobson has pointed out that only the three of them leave the furnace. Christ remains, ready to help the rest of us in our trials by fire.

We will not whine!

One aspect of the story may not impress you as much as it does me. Other administrators have told me how weary they too have grown of people's whining when things don't go their way. They gripe about their pay, complain about the workload, moan about being so misunderstood, bellyache because their overseers make life so difficult. Then there are the excuses. They missed their deadline because . . . They would have done a better job if it hadn't been for . . .

And now I'm whining! Unfairly, too. The truth is that most of the people I have worked with are producers. As fellow Christians, they and I are yoked together in a great mission and they give their all. So I'm not talking about them. But there are a few others . . .

I like E. Ray Jones' perspective on this subject. "Cotton" is my longtime friend. I followed him in the E. 38th Street Christian Church pastorate in Indianapolis in 1973, where I learned firsthand how much a gifted minister can bless a church. Then in later years, during his tenure in Clearwater, Florida, we annually bunked in the same guest apartment while teaching our one-week intensive courses in the graduate program at Kentucky Christian College. I appreciate his no-nonsense approach to the ministry. Here's his story:

"I was in Omaha, Nebraska, in March teaching a graduate course for the Cincinnati Christian Seminary. Because of the storm, my flight to Atlanta was canceled. I was put on a flight to Chicago where I stayed for eight hours. I then boarded a flight to Orlando, Florida, arriving at 1:00 A.M., only to find that the flight to Tampa had long since been canceled. I was told by the airlines that there was 'no room' in Orlando. So I spent the night sleeping on the floor in the Orlando airport. I caught a 7:30 flight out of Orlando, landed in Tampa at 8:15, and drove to Clearwater. A little haggard, but otherwise unscarred, I preached at the 8:45 service Sunday morning.

"Now who was to blame for all this? Well, it could be God, because after all it is His weather. It could be the airlines, because they are in the flight business. It is their business to get me where I was going. It could be the airport's problem because they did not have enough equipment to clear the runways. Or it could be the Seminary. After all, they sent me to Nebraska.

"To be honest about it, it was my fault. Some twenty years ago I chose the path that led me to the situation I faced that weekend. When I made the choice to teach in graduate school, I put in motion those events that resulted in the problem I encountered on the weekend of March 14, 1993."[2]

No whining. Just an acceptance of the consequences of his own decision.

Shadrach, Meshach, and Abednego also made a decision long before their run-in with Nebuchadnezzar. Their choice? To be faithful to God, no matter what. The consequence of that long-ago choice? The furnace. Who else could they blame? And anyway, what good would complaining do?

Everyone knows we have to pay for our bad choices in life. What we forget is the price to be paid for our good ones.

We will put our lives where our mouths are.

You've heard that wise counsel of Yogi Berra? "When you come to a fork in the road—take it." I like it even better than another helpful bit of insight, this from Woody Allen (his opening lines in his essay, "My Speech to the Graduates"). "More than any other time in history, mankind faces a crossroad. One path leads to despair and utter hopelessness. The other, to total extinction. Let us pray we have the wisdom to choose correctly." Allen's is a more sophisticated version of the familiar "caught between a rock and a hard place" that we heard so often when we lived in Tennessee.

Whatever you call it, Shadrach, Meshach, and Abednego are there. For them the time has come to put their lives where their mouths are. At some point you have to stop talking about your faith and actually live up to it.

You may know the delightful story told on physicist Max Planck. He died and went to Heaven where, our informant confides, he was met at the gate by St. Peter, who invited him in. Aware of his academic background, Peter held out a choice. "Professor Planck, this door goes to the Kingdom of Heaven, while that door leads to a discussion about the Kingdom of Heaven." Guess which one he chose? Ah, how academicians love to discuss. Do you suppose the professor was at least partially Greek? The Bible reports that *all the Athenians and the foreigners who lived there spent their time doing nothing but talking about and listening to the latest ideas* (Acts 17:21).

This isn't just a problem at Athens, of course. All academe is dedicated to "processing," which is, in one form or another, an ideal method of delaying a decision by forming a committee. That way no one has to be finally responsible for the consequences. Sir Barnett Cocks has astutely observed, "A committee is a cul-de-sac down which ideas are lured and then quietly strangled." A committee legitimizes talk in place of action.

So what is your choice?

When in midlife you turn your soul over to God, much to the disapproval of your wife (who married you in your carefree pre-Christian days), what is your stand?

When your employer or supervisor insists on your doing what clearly violates your moral and ethical values, what is your stand?

When you read of Patrick Henry's famous declaration for independence, "Give me liberty or give me death," can you imagine yourself ready to sacrifice everything you have, even your life, for the sake of anything? What is your stand?

How willing are you to put your life where your mouth is?

Now we can turn to the climax of the narrative. This story has a happy ending. Our heroes are in fact saved.

Rescued from danger

Then Nebuchadnezzar said, "Praise be to the God of Shadrach, Meshach and Abednego, who has sent his angel and rescued his servants! They trusted in him and defied the king's command and were willing to give up their lives rather than serve or worship any god except their own God."

Even Nebuchadnezzar has to acknowledge the miracle. The men could not have saved themselves. *God sent his angel and rescued his servants!* They defied the king, trusted God, and God delivered them from danger.

As a longtime pastor I have been privileged to listen to many tales of deliverance. In hushed, awed tones the rescued speak of life-threatening illnesses overcome, death-defying escapes, extraordinary rescues too bizarre to be merely coincidental. You cannot convince these who have faced death squarely and been spared that God was not in their rescue.

At our all-family vacation this year, two of our dearest friends told their story. Though their adventure took place many years ago, they still speak with awe of the night their fuel-dry airplane went down on the foggy Oregon coast and they walked away to talk about it.

Ted shakes his head. "It was my fault," he admits. He was the trained pilot. He made one of the cardinal mistakes—he didn't have a backup plan in case something went wrong. He knew he was stretching the limits of the plane's fuel capacity when he left the Willamette Valley for Tillamook. But the sky was clear and the winds were calm and he didn't foresee any problem.

But as he and George crossed over the coastal mountains, their vision was enshrouded in dense fog. They couldn't see where to land. They lost their way. Telling our family this story just weeks after young John Kennedy's plane crashed in the Atlantic, they said Kennedy's accident caused them to relive the terror of that night. They could have met the same fate. In the fog in the dark it is very easy to become so disoriented you can't tell up from down. What made it worse for Ted, he said, was that George was and is his best friend. If he had died because of Ted's poor judgment, well . . .

Finally, in desperation as the plane coughed on the last drop of fuel, Ted was forced to bring the plane in for a landing. He couldn't find a landing strip, he didn't know where on the coast he was, but he had no choice. As the crippled plane drifted downward Ted could make out a sand spit in the waters below. Not a good landing spot, but at least there were no trees or boulders.

The landing was not smooth. The plane quickly bogged down in the soft sand, stood on its nose, and flipped over. But Ted and George walked away unharmed. They were soon rescued by a man who had heard the motor and eventually seen the lights of the descending plane. He picked them up in his boat—and recognized them. That's when they learned that they had come down within just a few miles of home.

Ted and George are both elders in their church. You don't have to ask them whether they believe God is real. His hand rescued them and they have lived to serve Him ever since.

Then the king promoted Shadrach, Meshach and Abednego in the province of Babylon. And like Ted and

George, they lived to serve. God's rescue operation is a success. The men's faith has been vindicated. Their reward is a promotion—to a higher level of responsibility.

They have been saved to serve.

And you?

---

[1]Friedrich, Otto. "Every Man Was a Hero." *Time* (5/28/84):16

[2]Jones, E. Ray. "The Minister Muses," *Clearwater Christian,* June 23, 1993.

GEAR UP

1. What is most disturbing to you in the words spoken by Shadrach, Meshach, and Abednego in Daniel 3:16-18?

2. What verse in Psalm 31:1-5 would be most difficult for you to pray if you were in a situation where standing up for God meant certain death? Explain your answer.

3. How does the commitment of these men challenge you in your commitment to God?

4. Do you have Christian friends who support you? What do they do for you that you can't do for yourself?

5. How can a supportive friend help you stand firm for God in a situation where you are tempted to compromise?

6. Ecclesiastes 4:12 says, *Though one may be overpowered, two can defend themselves. A cord of three strands is not quickly broken.* How has this proved true in your life?

7. Friends are one of God's greatest gifts. There is, however, *a friend who sticks closer than a brother* (Proverbs 18:24). How has God proved His words to you, *"Never will I leave you; never will I forsake you"* (Hebrews 13:5)?

8. Have you discovered that there is often a price to be paid for the good choices you make? Explain your answer.

9. What might it cost you to serve God with all your heart?

86 *Rescued!*

10. Complete the following sentence: Recognizing that I am called to serve makes me want to . . .

11. A plane crashes somewhere in the world almost every month, and in many cases, Christians die. We can safely assume that in some of these cases, Christians have prayed for a safe flight. Does this shake your faith in God? Why, or why not?

12. On the other hand, many of us can relate experiences where our lives seem to have been saved in a miraculous manner. Dr. Lawson's conclusion is, "We have been saved to serve." If this is true, are you fulfilling the purpose of your life?

13. How can you prepare yourself to be a person God can use to serve others?

7
RESCUED FROM
A WICKED PLOT
Esther 4:1-17; 5–7

QUEEN ESTHER'S is a Cinderella story, a classic rags to riches tale, but with a Middle Eastern twist. When King Xerxes deposed the beautiful Queen Vashti for snubbing him when he summoned her to his banquet (he wanted to show her off to his guests), he asked his advisors how he should replace her. Following their counsel he ordered a search for his kingdom's most beautiful young virgins. They would be added to his harem and plied with lotions and perfumed ointments to make them alluring enough to please the king. From among these charmers Xerxes would select his next queen.

The winner, as you already know, was Esther, the orphaned cousin of the Jew Mordecai. She was ravishing (*lovely in form and features,* the Bible says). She immediately caught the eye of Hegai, harem-master, who gave her the benefit of his years of studying his king's preferences. Esther was his favorite; he wanted her above all others to be the next queen, so he personally took charge. He carefully supervised twelve months of beauty treatments (including six months with oil of myrrh and six with perfumes and cosmetics). Her natural beauty combined with his inside knowledge of kingly tastes and exotic allurements transformed the humble maid into an irresistible beauty fit for the king.

There was only one problem. Esther had a hidden identity.

88 *Rescued!*

Obeying her cousin, she did not reveal her nationality. Hegai had no idea he was promoting a Jew to a Persian court.

Now the king was attracted to Esther more than to any of the other women, and she won his favor and approval more than any of the other virgins. So he set a royal crown on her head and made her queen instead of Vashti. And the king gave a great banquet, Esther's banquet, for all his nobles and officials. He proclaimed a holiday throughout the provinces and distributed gifts with royal liberality.

So far so good. Esther's life was a dream come true. All went well until Mordecai got himself into trouble. Sitting at the king's gate as was his custom (so he could keep track of Esther's welfare), he discovered a plot. A couple of the king's officers planned to assassinate King Xerxes. He quickly reported them to Queen Esther, who in turn passed the word to the monarch. The would-be assassins were summarily hanged. She gave Mordecai the credit.

His new notoriety placed Mordecai at risk. The king's arrogant favorite, Haman, became outraged when sometime later Mordecai refused to kneel to him or otherwise pay him obeisance, as the royal officials did. Whether the reason was jealousy or spite or whatever, these officials reported Mordecai's stubbornness to Haman, to see what he would do. They also let it leak that Mordecai was a Jew.

The enraged Haman would have his revenge, not just on Mordecai, but on all the Jews in Xerxes's kingdom. He incited the king to violence by reporting on *a certain people dispersed and scattered among the peoples in all the provinces of your kingdom whose customs are different from those of all other people and who do not obey the king's laws; it is not in the king's best interest to tolerate them.* His counsel was fatal: *If it pleases the king, let a decree be issued to destroy them, and I will put ten thousand talents of silver into the royal treasury for the men who carry out this business.*

And it was so.

The order was dispatched to each province and language group in the kingdom: Let the entire race of the Jews, their old and young, men and women and children—all of them be put to death and their goods plundered.

This is the sordid background to Esther's story. It explains why Mordecai, tearing his clothes and donning the sackcloth and ashes of mourning, sent word to Esther to appeal to the king on her people's behalf.

Esther was frightened. One simply did not enter the presence of the king without his summons. To do so was to die. She instructed the messenger to tell her cousin she couldn't do it.

Mordecai's answer must have both chilled and inspired Esther: *"Do not think that because you are in the king's house you alone of all the Jews will escape. For if you remain silent at this time, relief and deliverance for the Jews will arise from another place, but you and your father's family will perish. And who knows but that you have come to royal position for such a time as this?"*

Note Mordecai's remarkable faith. This is a severe crisis; a whole race of people is threatened. But Mordecai has no doubt God will deliver the Jews from destruction. Their fate is not his primary worry. Hers is. If she fails to act, she will certainly die.

But deliverance will come to the Jews, with or without Esther's help.

The probing question

Who knows but that you have come to royal position for such a time as this?

Many centuries later the apostle Paul would grasp the same sense of God's time management that motivates Mordecai. *For we are God's workmanship, created in Christ Jesus to do good works, which God prepared in advance for us to do,* Paul writes in Ephesians 2:10. God has prepared us through Christ so that we can accomplish good works for Him. Life has purpose. We have been saved by Christ's atoning act (*For it is by grace you have been saved, through faith—and this not from yourselves, it is the gift of God,* 2:8). We didn't save ourselves (*not by works, so that no one can boast,* 2:9). God did the work and we received the grace . . .

for such a time as this.

For a moment Esther's fate seems to be entirely in her own hands. No one, not even her cousin, can force her to risk her life for her fellow Jews. No one in the king's court even knows her racial identity. She can turn her back on the beleaguered people and live in splendid comfort for the rest of her days.

But to what end? For what purpose? This is her moment. As far as her cousin is concerned, God has been preparing her all along for just such a moment. If she is safe for the time being, it is *for such a time as this,* to do this good work.

Have you ever asked yourself Mordecai's question? Have you ever been faced with a decision so momentous that it seemed as if everything in your life up to that minute had been preparation for it? As if everything afterward would be governed by the choice you were about to make?

My "moment" was far less dramatic than Esther's, but it was as significant for me. It came in 1990. (Please forgive me for returning to the autobiographical sketch in chapter 5. This part of the story is, in a sense, my defining moment, and I return to it often.)

In 1973 I resigned as vice president of Milligan College in Tennessee to accept the call to become senior minister of East 38th Street Christian Church in Indianapolis. To a casual observer this appeared to be a normal midlife career adjustment.

It didn't seem so to me. Let me tell you why.

As a teenager I received the call to preach. Following the call, I turned down a scholarship to study chemistry at the University of Oregon and instead enrolled at Northwest Christian College to pursue ministerial studies. Even before graduating, I became the founding minister of a church in Tigard, a suburb of Portland. While serving there for six years, I obtained three degrees, taught high school, married, and fathered two children. At twenty-seven, though, I sincerely believed God was calling me from that rich preaching experience to college teaching, so I resigned and moved the family across the continent to Tennessee, where for eight years I was a college professor, completing my doctorate at Vanderbilt along the way.

But then came the 1973 move to Indianapolis. I had never been more certain of anything than that God was calling me away from Milligan, where as vice president I was being groomed to succeed to the presidency in a few years, and away from college teaching, which was richly rewarding. What made no sense at the time were the sacrifices I had caused my wife to make in order for me to complete my doctorate—a requirement for academic leadership, but not needed (and in some ways not even helpful) in pastoral ministry.

What was going on in my life? Why should I once more uproot our family (by now there were three children) from our secure, comfortable life in the hills of East Tennessee for the far more strenuous demands of an urban ministry? And what about the now superfluous doctorate? Friends and family must have questioned my judgment. More than one comment was made about the male midlife crisis coming rather early in my case. I had no satisfactory answer to give them because I didn't understand what was going on either. I just had this strong sense of God's leading and my need to be obedient. How often I have thanked God for a patient wife whose loyalty I must have tested to the maximum.

For seventeen years my questions went unanswered. Not until 1990 did it make sense. That was when Pacific Christian College called me to the joint ministry that was to be mine for nine years: president of Pacific Christian College in Fullerton, California and senior minister of the Central Christian Church in Mesa, Arizona. Now all the pieces of the puzzle came together—the apprenticeship in that earliest church, the years of college teaching and administration, the sacrifices for the doctorate, the unceasing demands of that urban ministry, and the relocation to the desert of Arizona in the college's constituent area.

So now I know. God gave me those years as preparation for the larger ministry to come. He knew way back then that *such a time as this* lay ahead and He wanted me to be ready.

A haunting question remains. Now that I'm in my sixties and have left the twenty-year Mesa ministry behind to concentrate on leading what now has become Hope International University, has the full answer been given yet? Is there still another time, another task for which I am even now being prepared? Will there be another defining moment? You and I can name persons who achieved their greatest work after they were older than I am now. Could I be one?

Could you?

Mordecai's question certainly puts education in its proper place, doesn't it? Do you recall how most of us as students badgered our teachers? "Do I have to know this?" "Will it be on the test?" "Why should I have to learn this stuff? I'm never going to use it in real life!" We had to learn it anyway, because our teachers understood something we didn't really grasp until much later. We were being prepared for our time to come, outfitted for purposes we couldn't even vaguely comprehend then.

If anything, this educator is less satisfied than ever with American higher education's trend toward vocational *training* as opposed to more traditional *education*. Training is practical, job-related, and helpful for a career. Education often seems irrelevant, abstract, dominated by those infamous dead white men who have been so much maligned in recent years. When I think back on the "practical" training in many of my classes, I am astonished at how much I have forgotten and how much I wouldn't dare apply today. The practical quickly passes. What I have retained, on the other hand, is precisely the material I griped about learning way back then. That "stuff" that schools of arts and sciences teach—that's what I am turning to these days. I can pick up the "how-tos" off the Internet; wrestling with the questions that perplexed the giants of intellectual history, on the other hand, remains a satisfying avocation.

Well, I seem to have digressed. My lifelong fascination with questions of meaning and purpose has surfaced again. Let me excuse myself by admitting my passion for helping men and women prepare for the real defining moments of life. Anyone can get a job and pursue a trade. Not everyone, though, is ready *for such a time as this.* In our rapidly changing culture, to be qualified to do a particular job isn't good enough, especially with experts telling us that most workers will change vocations (not just employers) at least five times during their working years.

Our real concern as educators has to be to equip our students for their *time.* Will they have the psychological, emotional, mental, and spiritual strength, will they have grown wise enough, deep enough, so that when their moment comes, they can *act*?

A friend recently sent me a tidbit he had downloaded from the Internet. It's about three friends who die in a car crash. They find themselves at the gates of Heaven, where St. Peter asks them a question: "When you are in your casket and friends and family are mourning over you, what would you like to hear them say about you?"

The first man had his answer ready. "I would like to hear them say that I was a great doctor of my time, and a great family man."

The second took a little longer, but he also had his values clearly in mind. "I would like to hear that I was a wonderful husband and schoolteacher who made a huge difference in our children of tomorrow."

The third was right to the point. "I would like to hear them say, 'LOOK!! HE'S MOVING!!!'"

It's a good joke, but if he were serious it would be a sad commentary on his life, wouldn't it? Had Queen Esther's primary desire been to keep moving, to preserve her own life at the cost of her people's, we would know nothing about her. She would have faded into oblivion like the billions of

94 *Rescued!*

other souls who saved their own skins but never fulfilled the purpose for which God, in His wonderful sense of timing, had prepared them.

Fortunately she was ready, and she acted.

The courageous answer

The narrative is so understated. What emotions must have coursed through Esther's heart, what hesitations, resolutions, what sadness and longing, what near despair at the prospect of losing everything she has worked so hard for? Does she resent her cousin for his unreasonable demand? Is she proud to be the chosen spokesperson for her race? Does she rue her certain loss of status? None of this insight is given us. We can't help marveling at her great courage, though, as she sends the word back to Mordecai: *"Go, gather together all the Jews who are in Susa, and fast for me. Do not eat or drink for three days, night or day. I and my maids will fast as you do. When this is done, I will go to the king, even though it is against the law. And if I perish, I perish."*

"And if I perish, I perish." "Since this is the moment for which God has prepared me, then the consequences are in His hands, not mine, so I will act and leave the rest up to Him. But you must help me, my dear cousin. Those on whose behalf I am daring to enter the presence of the king, they must help me, also. Get them to fast on my behalf; my maids and I will be fasting also."

It is often pointed out that in the entire book of Esther, God's name is not even mentioned. Some commentators have wondered how such a secular book could be among the sacred treasures of Scripture that constitute our Bible. But God is there: He is there in the purposeful timing we have been discussing; He is there in the fasting, the Jewish rite of preparation, a time-honored method of getting ready to go before the face of God and of invoking His benediction.

The absence of God's name in the book of Esther is hard

for people who love dropping God's name to understand. They do not seem to comprehend that those who walk most intimately with God often do not feel the need to drop His name frequently. But they know He is, and that He is "there," and that their times are in His hands. Thus Esther.

What seems to be an act of fatalism on Esther's part is more accurately read as a faithful young woman's dependence on the will of God. Through prayer and fasting she and her people express their trust in God; if He has purposes that mean her death, she is prepared to die. If, on the other hand, He sees fit to rescue her and her people, she is prepared to live.

Os Guinness recounts in his recent book, *The Call,* meeting a prominent businessman at a conference near Oxford University. He was impressed with the man's strong facial features and evident signs of success. He listened as the man recounted his fortunate career, the money he made, and the fact that with so much money he never had to do anything he didn't like. He could hire others instead. In the American sense of the words, he had arrived. But he then confessed that he could never hire anyone to do something that mattered more than anything else to him: "find my own sense of purpose and fulfillment." He said he'd give anything he had to discover that. Guinness adds that in his thirty years of public speaking and countless conversations that issue had come up more often than any other.

His experience resonates with my own. Success is never enough. Only significance satisfies, and that is always dependent upon a strong sense of purpose.

How can the businessman find that purpose? What could he do that would bring genuine fulfillment?

The answer is another question. For what would you be willing to give it all up? You have great wealth. What's it good for? Who is it good for?

Most of us will never accumulate the riches this man has, but the question of purpose is the same: For what are you willing to give it up? Or, the question I've asked more than one young man who is under fire because of some stand he has taken: Are you willing to be fired for this one?

The frivolous woman describing the beautiful dress she found on a shopping spree proclaims, "It's to die for." She doesn't mean it, of course.

But Esther does mean it. It's to die for.

When we have discovered what's worth dying for, then we know what we are living for. As far as Esther is concerned, her people are worth dying for.

In V. S. Pritchett's provocative essay, "An Émigré," he calls an emigrant's isolation from his homeland and people a "daily evil." What makes it evil is that he has lost what Pritchett calls the "main ground of the moral life." That moral foundation is the realization that "we do not live until we live in others." In Esther's decision to live for her people, even if it means dying for them, she finds life.

Contrast Esther's decision with that of Innokenty and Dotnara, described so poignantly by Aleksandr Solzhenitsyn in *The First Circle*. Their philosophy, he says, was "only one life." They lived for the moment and for each other. "They tried every new and strange fruit. They learned the taste of every fine cognac, learned to tell Rhone wines from the wines of Corsica, to know all the wines from all the vineyards of the earth. To wear clothes of every kind. To dance every dance. To swim at every resort. To play tennis and to sail a boat. To attend an act or two of every unusual play. To leaf through every sensational book.

"For six years, the best of their youth, they gave each other everything. Those were the years when mankind was racked by partings, dying in the front lines and under the ruins of cities, when adults gone mad were grabbing crumbs of black bread from the hands of children. But none of the world's grief had touched Innokenty and Dotnara."

Their justification for their self-centered existence? "After all, we have only one life!"[1] Without leaving their homeland they have isolated themselves from their own people. They have lost what Pritchett calls in his essay "the main ground of the moral life." Unwilling to live for others, they aren't fully alive in spite of their protest, "We have only one life."

One life is all Esther has also. She is ready, however, to lay it down for her people. As Solzhenitsyn describes them, Innokenty and Dotnara have chosen to have no people. Their lives are defined by the their entertainment and accessories, their superficial samplings of books and plays, their deliberate ignoring of the world's grief.

They are alone and empty.

And Esther? She saves the lives of her people. The young woman who entered the beauty contest and won the king's hand risks everything for her people. That is the difference, isn't it, between a commoner and a real queen?

---

[1]Solzhenitsyn, Aleksandr. *The First Circle*. New York: Harper & Row Publishers, Inc., 1968.

GEAR UP

1. Have you ever been asked to do something that you felt you just couldn't do? What was it?

2. Why do you think Mordecai was so sure that Esther should be the one to go to the king?

3. Why do you think he said she would surely die if she refused to go?

4. Think back to Esther's early years. How might God have used them to shape her into a woman He could use during this crisis (see Esther 2:5-7)?

5. What about you? What good work do you think God prepared for you to do?

6. What has God done to prepare you for your work?

7. Do you think there still may be other tasks ahead for you? What might these be and how might He be preparing you today to do them?

8. Dr. Lawson wrote that success is never enough, only significance is. Have you known anyone who has discovered lasting fulfillment? How did they go about finding it?

100 *Rescued!*

9. Another question is even more searching. What things in your life are worth dying for?

10. Think back to Jesus' death on the cross. What and who did Jesus consider worth dying for?

11. How has His great love been reflected in His followers down through the ages?

12. How would you like to see the love of Jesus reflected in your life?

8
RESCUED FROM
FEAR

Mark 4:35-41

THIS CHAPTER is the exception in our study. The others are about courage in the face of danger or deprivation. In this episode on the Sea of Galilee, courage is decidedly missing. Fear, not boldness, consumes Jesus' disciples.

It's about fear . . . and faith.

"Teacher, don't you care if we drown?"

They don't expect a miracle out of Jesus; they resent His sleep. They want Him to wake up and worry with them!

Theirs isn't the mindless panic of the ignorant, either. These men have grown up in Galilee; several are fishermen. They love the lake that dominates their lives, that provides their living. But they also have a healthy respect for its volatile temperament, the sudden squalls screaming down from Mount Hermon, whipping the glassy surface into a riot of steep peaks and deep valleys, threatening lives and breaking vessels too fragile for its fury. From childhood they have heard the tales of men who sailed from shore in calm seas but never returned, tossed by the suddenly angry swells to their premature burials.

The disciples are afraid. They have every right to be.

Or so they think. Jesus is of a different opinion. *"Why are you so afraid? Do you still have no faith?"*

What does He expect of them?

John says, *"Perfect love drives out fear"* (1 John 4:18). Scripture doesn't say, in so many words, "Perfect faith drives out fear," yet this seems to be what Jesus is implying here. "If you had faith, you wouldn't be afraid of this storm. Because you don't, you are scared when there's no need to be."

Isn't this also what the psalmist means when he sings, *Even though I walk through the valley of the shadow of death, I will fear no evil, for you are with me; your rod and your staff, they comfort me* (23:4)? Or again in Psalm 46:1-3: *God is our refuge and strength, an ever-present help in trouble. Therefore we will not fear, though the earth give way and the mountains fall into the heart of the sea, though its waters roar and foam and the mountains quake with their surging.*

There is something very practical about such faith. Jesus is not inquiring about their intellectual grasp of Scripture or the maturity of their theological understanding. He wonders why they haven't yet learned to trust.

If Jesus were to question them as the waves were pounding and the rain was pouring on them—but who can carry on a conversation in such peril?—they could have satisfied Him regarding their minds' acceptance of the faith of their fathers. They would assure Him they believe in God. They are not only descendants of Abraham but are active proponents of the Jewish faith as a set of beliefs and moral guidelines. Nothing is wrong with their minds.

But Jesus has a deeper concern. What has happened to their hearts?

I know what He's driving at, don't you? As a very nervous boy standing before my home congregation I confessed my belief (genuine then, genuine now) that Jesus is the Christ, the Son of the living God. I was then baptized in the name of the Father, Son, and Holy Spirit. I was welcomed into the bosom of the congregation and taught the way of the Lord more perfectly by godly Sunday school teachers and a brilliant preacher. I went to Bible college and studied for the ministry. Since my ordination I have preached for more than forty years. I believe.

But I don't always trust.

When the storms arise and threaten, a familiar feeling of panic grips me. I have even been known to cry out, "Don't You care that I'm drowning here?" In the classroom, in the pulpit, I can present a strong case for the faith. On the storm-tossed sea, I forget my own lessons.

Perhaps that is why, as I have grown older, I have deliberately done some things that cause my friends to doubt my maturity. When I turned sixty, for example, our adopted son Brian, and our son-in-law Ed kidnapped me (with Joy going along as accomplice and photographer), tossed me in the car, and drove me to Eloi, Arizona. Maybe the boys had grown tired of hearing me say, "Someday I'm going to. . . ." They decided it was put up or shut up time. My birthday present was a sky dive. We jumped out of a plane at thirteen thousand feet, free-fell to five thousand, then opened parachutes and drifted down the rest of the way. It was exhilarating.

It didn't quite compare, though, to my adventure as a fifty-five-year-old in New Zealand. Just before the tour group left for down under, Joy told me she didn't think I should go. She told me she had been watching "Good Morning America," which had run a series on New Zealand. In one of the segments the focus was on two activities that originated there: hang gliding and bungee jumping. She knew that three times a couple of friends and I had driven to San Diego to hang glide off the ocean cliffs, but all three times a windless day stopped us. She was afraid I might try that or, even worse, jump off a bridge.

I assured her she didn't need to worry. And she didn't need to. My tour-leading partner Mike and I already had decided that if the bus went anywhere near the bridge where this craze originated, we would try it. But she didn't need to worry.

As it turned out, our tour took us right to the bridge. Our

driver had tried the jump himself and encouraged us to take the plunge. But on the morning we were to do so, I was still battling a stubborn cold (it was winter down south) and had several sermons to preach at a convention in the days ahead, so I reluctantly had to encourage Mike to go ahead without me.

At the bridge the rest of the group went to the bluff overlooking the river, but I walked with Mike to encourage him as he signed up. While they weighed him and did the paperwork, I paced the floor, debating. Finally I decided that I needed to join him. Three steps in my reasoning still stand out:

1) "Well, Lawson, you are always preaching about faith..." I confess there was some fear involved. It's not every day that you jump from one hundred forty-three feet above the river with nothing to save you but a large rubber band.

2) "You're fifty-five years old and it's been a good life." What if the cord should snap? People have died doing this stunt. What if you should be next? (One of our fellow tourists, a delightful lady in her seventies, had said to us the day before, "Do you know what they call a bungee jumper? A dope on a rope." She didn't know then that the tour director was about to become one.)

3) "You'll probably never get another opportunity." This was the deciding argument.

Why am I confessing to you this trivial event in my life? Because, believe it or not, this was a moment of *faith* (trust) for me. I had known many others, such as when our daughter was dangerously sick and we were finally able to turn her over to God for healing. Or when I was fighting my way back to sanity after our son died, or counting on God to help me through a crisis in marriage, or accepting His guidance when as a pastor I had to brave a potentially treacherous church emergency, with little to keep me going but faith (trust) in God.

My momentary internal wrestling match over whether to jump or not jump off that bridge was, as I said, a trivial debate, certainly when compared with the real spiritual struggles in my life. I'm grateful for something Harry Emerson Fosdick taught me early in my Christian walk. He wrote that most Christians know about the faith of the great believers but not about their inner struggles. He mentioned William Lyon Phelps, who confessed, "My religious faith remains in possession of the field only after prolonged civil war with my naturally sceptical mind." And John Knox, the Scottish reformer, who remembered a "time when my soul knew anger, wrath, and indignation, which it conceived against God, calling all His promises in doubt." Increase Mather, the formidable Puritan preacher, went through a period when he was "greatly molested with temptations to atheism." Martin Luther, the intrepid Reformation leader, admitted a time when "for more than a week, Christ was wholly lost. I was shaken by desperation and blasphemy against God."

There may be solid saints whose spiritual tranquillity has never been shaken by the tempests of doubt and indecision, whose trust in God has never been threatened, but I don't know any. Fosdick's recommendation is that we make our way "honestly through with [our] disbeliefs," staying with it until finally we begin to "doubt our doubts, disbelieve our disbeliefs."[1] His is good counsel.

Jesus is asking the right question: *"Do you still have no faith?"* Do you understand that your fright is not caused by the weather but by your own lack of trust?

Think for a moment about your own fears, and whether you have the faith to cast them out. If you are like most of us, your list of phobias will begin with snakes and spiders, move on to speaking in public or entering a roomful of strangers, and include all kinds of natural disasters, fear of losing control of your life, having your secrets discovered, and being rejected.

Some of us are concerned that today's youngsters will have an even greater struggle with their fears than we old-timers do, because in this frightening society they are being taught to distrust everyone. Don't talk to strangers, parents instruct their children, even though, as radio personality Dennis Prager admonishes, a child's chance of being kidnapped by a stranger is virtually nil. The real threats are adult relatives and acquaintances. Perhaps they should talk only to strangers!

It's about fear . . . and selfishness.

"... if _we_ drown?"

The question is whether the disciples are including Jesus in the _we_. Are they speaking of Jesus _and_ themselves or Jesus _over against_ themselves? "You can drown if You want to, Jesus, but don't You care if _we_ drown?"

Their self-centeredness is understandable. Self-preservation is a basic human instinct, perhaps _the_ basic instinct, but it's not the prettiest one to see in action, and it certainly doesn't do anything for the panicky one's peace of mind.

I have read this story more times than I can count. I have checked it out in other versions. No matter how I seek to hear something else in the disciples' voices, their tone always sounds like resentment. "How can You be so calm? How dare You sleep when we're so frightened, or when we could use another hand with the bailing?" How can You be so, so, so different?

Resentment feeds on fear. Fear we will drown, will not be liked, will be shown up by someone better, will be discovered, will be unappreciated or diminished, will be finally defeated, will be rejected. What is it but fear that fosters resentment—unless it's selfishness? Why aren't things arranged more for my convenience and comfort? Why aren't you meeting my personal needs _right now_? We laugh as Professor Higgins huffs his song in _My Fair Lady,_ "Why can't a woman . . . be more like a man?" because we recognize both the absurdity and the pervasiveness of the question. What is self-centeredness but the desire for everyone else to be and do what I want them to? Having placed myself at the center of the universe, I expect to be served. And here's Jesus, ignoring me! Sleeping. Oblivious to my peril. (Each disciple is looking out for himself, a part of the group only to the extent that it's to his advantage.)

So they complain. Yet if Jesus were more like them, wouldn't they be even more disturbed?

That is the problem with egocentricity. The self that lives for self finds satisfaction only in the self. Everybody else, even the Son of God, is an irritant.

It's about faith . . . and a good night's sleep.

The disciples are terrified. Jesus, on the other hand, sleeps. It's about faith, isn't it, this ability to sleep in a storm? The great scientist Johannes Kepler said the great question of his life was to know whether he could find God, "whom I can almost grasp with my own hands in looking at the universe," also in himself. Was he searching for the Holy Spirit who indwells the believer, the Spirit whom Christ promised as a comforter? Trusting the Spirit makes possible a sound sleep in the storm.

In one of his books Paul Tournier says that faith always involves risk. He then lists the risks demanded of the faithful:

- of being criticized for . . . unfaithfulness
- of failing—of being beaten in the battle of life
- of being let down if we try to love, to forgive, and to trust
- of losing the affection of a wife or husband or friend who isn't prepared to follow us
- of losing our independence, our claim not to be answerable to anyone else, even God
- of being found on the side of many other Christians who are properly open to criticism
- of having our faith used as a weapon against us
- of being led from one act of obedience to another, farther than we would have wished

- of having to make the final sacrifice
- of mistaking the divine call, or of mistaking God's guidance.

I would add one more to his catalog: the risk of getting what we thought we wanted and being deeply disappointed when we discover it doesn't deliver what it promised.

With so much at stake, how can anyone sleep? A good rest will elude us unless we really do believe that God is able to deliver us, that He will be there to catch us if we fall, and that the relationship with Him is both more sure and more satisfying than success or failure in any undertaking.

Humorist Garrison Keillor in his *We Are Still Married* declares that even a little faith will see you through. In fact, nothing except faith will do in times as corrupt and cynical as ours. "When the country goes temporarily to the dogs," he says, "cats must learn to be circumspect, walk on fences, sleep in trees, and have faith that all this woofing is not the last word."[2]

That's the point. No matter how threatening the tempest, how grave the risk, how scary the faith-walk, you can sleep when you are convinced that "all this woofing is not the last word." It is God who pronounces the final "Amen."

It's about fear . . . and worship

Perfect love casts out fear. Solid faith casts out fear. And, it must be added, a greater fear casts out fear.

At first the disciples feared the wind and the waves. At last they feared Jesus. A new fear—something more powerful than the wind and waves: *They were terrified and asked each other, "Who is this? Even the wind and the waves obey him!"*

You may have noticed how often the Bible exhorts us to "fear the Lord." When people fail to "fear the Lord" they give themselves over to sin of every description. Dostoyevsky said, "If God does not exist, then everything is permitted." Jean Paul Sartre, the French philosopher so popular in the turbulent sixties, calls Dostoyevsky's remark the starting point of existentialism. "Indeed," he adds, "everything is permissible if God does not exist, and as a result man is forlorn, because neither within him nor without does he find anything to cling to."[2]

Actress Jane Fonda appeared on a late-night talk show in the early seventies along with the Archbishop of Canterbury. The subject turned to Christian belief. The archbishop had just said something about the importance of Jesus for the contemporary world, to which Fonda, then in her most radical phase, responded with disbelief. The venerable clergyman went on in most ecclesiastical voice, "Well, He is the Son of God, you know." Miss Fonda would not be stifled. "Well, perhaps He is to you, but not to me," she retorted. "Either He is or He isn't," the archbishop answered

This is the final word, isn't it? If He is, then the proper response is worship. If He isn't, why bother?

The disciples have moved beyond demand, even beyond debate, to awe. Implicit in their spoken question *("Who is this?")* is a deeper one: "What will I do with Him?" *"The winds and waves obey him!"* Since they obey, how can I disobey?

They were terrified.

Matthew's Gospel recounts another terrorizing incident on this lake. Very late at night the disciples spot Jesus walking toward them—on the water. *"It's a ghost," they said, and cried out in fear.* Jesus immediately assures them they aren't seeing things and urges them to calm down. Bluff, blustery Peter challenges Him: *"Lord, if it's you, tell me to come to you on the water."*

Jesus calls his bluff. *"Come,"* He answers him. *Then Peter got down out of the boat, walked on the water and came toward Jesus.*

It is too good to last though. Peter takes his eyes off the Lord, looks at the threatening wind, gets scared and begins to sink, crying out as he does, *"Lord, save me!"*

You already know the story. Jesus pulls him up—and then

scolds him! *"You of little faith,"* he said, *"why did you doubt?"*

Peter and Jesus climb into the boat, and the wind becomes quiet. But the disciples don't. Instead, *those who were in the boat worshiped him* (Matthew 14:25-33).

From the terror they felt when they saw the apparition walking toward them to the fright that gripped Peter as he began to sink—to the worship. They are in the presence of someone at once more comforting and more frightening than ghosts or winds or seas. From fear . . . to worship.

The Bible says *the fear of the Lord is the beginning of wisdom* (Proverbs 9:10, KJV). The writer of Ecclesiastes, after having tasted all the world's goods and imbibed all its so-called wisdom, distills his counsel into a sentence: *Now all has been heard; here is the conclusion of the matter: Fear God and keep his commandments, for this is the whole duty of man* (12:13).

The rest is up to God.

---

[1] Fosdick, Harry Emerson. "The Importance of Doubting Our Doubts." *A Chorus of Witnesses*, ed. by Thomas G. Long and Cornelius Plantinga, Jr. Grand Rapids: William B. Eerdmans Publishing Co., 1994.

[2] Keillor, Garrison. Quoted in "Reflections." *Christianity Today.* January 10, 1994.

[3] Sartre, Jean Paul. *Existentialism.* Quoted in C. Stephen Evans, *Why Believe?* Grand Rapids: William B. Eerdmans Publishing Company, 1996.

GEAR UP

1. Describe a situation you've been in when you have doubted Jesus' care.

2. How did He respond to your fear and doubt?

3. Why do you think it is sometimes so hard for believers to apply biblical truth to their lives?

4. What do you see as the connection between fear and selfishness?

5. How has your own selfishness fostered fear in your heart?

6. Dr. Lawson asks, "What is self-centeredness but the desire for everyone else to be and do what I want them to?" Think back over the past few days; how have you expected others to serve you?

7. How does putting your faith in God have power to change your attitude?

8. Which of the categories of risks listed by Paul Tournier and Dr. Lawson (pp. 107, 108) holds your greatest fear?

9. How has that fear kept you from your enjoyment of Jesus?

10. What speaks to you most about the fearfulness of the disciples?

11. What did they need to do in order to move from fear to faith?

12. What do you need to do to move from fear to faith?

9
RESCUED FROM
SIN

Luke 7:36-50

WHEN YOU LEAF THROUGH a book of devotions or, in the case of us preachers, of illustrations, the labels are usually very clear. It's the same if you consult a topical dictionary. *Forgiveness, faith, love, gratitude, salvation, peace*—the topics announce themselves as independent entities, with meaning boundaries clearly defined.

When you read through the Bible, however, the entities are seldom so independent; categories slip and slide into one another, and you discover yourself starting in one direction but before long you have doubled back or taken an unexpected detour on a tangent that expands the original topic far beyond the meaning you've previously assigned it.

This chapter, for example, is supposed to be about forgiveness of sin. The assigned Scripture reaches its climax with Jesus' welcome words, *"Your sins are forgiven."* But even this brief passage requires the careful student to look more deeply into the relation of forgiveness to faith, of faith to love, of love to gratitude, of gratitude to salvation, of salvation to peace, and of peace to forgiveness—and of each of them to all the others. At the end of our study we'll be holding a bouquet of blessings that go by the name "forgiven."

Unforgiving

The religious leaders are the foils in this episode in Simon's house (Luke 7:36-50). If Jesus represents the spirit of forgiveness, these men stand for the spirit of condemnation. They would condemn people to the consequences of their sin. With these Pharisees (I use the term somewhat tentatively, having learned how unfair it is to categorize all Pharisees as pharisaical) arrogance, judgmentalism, and ingratitude foster a hardness of heart. They would dismiss the intruding woman from their presence if they dared. Knowing the woman's history, they are quick to condemn Jesus. Good people don't associate with such a person.

As far as Jesus is concerned though, it is they, not the woman, who deserve censoring. Of what are they guilty? Read the text carefully. Would you agree with me in inferring from the passage, they are at least guilty

  • of being inhospitable: "*You did not give me any water for my feet . . .*"
  • of rudeness: "*You did not give me a kiss . . .*"
  • of inattention: "*You did not put oil on my head . . .*"
  • of not caring about Him: "*for she loved much.*"
  • (by implication) of a lack of faith: *Jesus said to the woman, "Your faith has saved you . . ."*
  • and, as their carping has already demonstrated, of lack of peace: "*Jesus said to the woman: "[You] go in peace."*
  • therefore, of not enjoying forgiveness: *Then Jesus said to her, "Your sins are forgiven."*

Am I being unfair? Am I reading too much into the text? Is there a case to be made for these religious leaders, so sure of their superiority, so contemptuous of Jesus for consorting with such a woman? As my tone indicates, I think their unforgiving spirit is pretty evident to any reader.

And yet, and yet—what can *we* say, we who can be pretty critical of the Pharisees yet blind to our own spiritual arrogance? If we had been at Simon's, what would we have thought of this woman? Apparently she has crashed the party, she has certainly violated a basic social code by mixing with the men and lavishing her attention on Jesus, and she seems oblivious to the stir she is causing. Put yourself in Simon's place. What would you have done with the woman? Or said about her?

Being socially correct, which I was always taught to be, carries its own risks with it. Even in my advancing maturity I still hear the voice of my mother asking, as she did so frequently in my youth, "What will the neighbors think?" This isn't always a bad question, until you consider the power it gives the neighbors!

My mother's question was her way of enforcing conventional wisdom. Conventional wisdom is whatever the in-group says it is, whether the group is the party in power, the overseers of the religious denomination, the arbiters of fashion—whatever group or person. No contradicting voice is raised in Simon's house; no colleague challenges the prevailing opinion: the woman is a sinner, the teacher is a phony. If He were genuine, He would know better than to associate with the likes of her.

Peter Gomes, Harvard's chaplain, offered prayer at President Reagan's second inauguration in 1985. Afterward someone in Washington asked him what his "friends in the People's Republic of Cambridge" would say of his unthinkable violation of Harvard's mostly Democratic bias. I don't know what the chaplain answered then, but he didn't have to wait long to find out what people thought. "I was at dinner, at a fashionable table, in a fashionable house, in a fashionable street, hard by this fashionable church, filled with people who pay others to feed the hungry and clothe the naked, and one lady said to me after the soup and after she had exhausted the limited supply of small talk, in sheer exasperation, "How *could* you?"[1]

How could he indeed? Dr. Gomes, an African American, replied that Mr. Lincoln freed the slaves and he felt he owed a debt to the Republican party (Mr. Lincoln's). She failed to see the humor in his retort.

He had done nothing wrong. He had just violated

Harvard's conventional wisdom. What would the neighbors think?

I wonder whether the good woman ever heard of Joseph Parker? He was the minister of City Temple in London at the end of the nineteenth century. He was undoubtedly a superior preacher, but what I have liked best about him is one impromptu comment he made in response to another lady who was as convinced of her righteousness as Dr. Gomes's antagonist. As Parker climbed the steps into his pulpit one Sunday morning a lady threw a piece of paper at him. Picking it up, he read a single word: "Fool."

"I have received many anonymous letters in my life," he told the congregation. "Previously they had been a text without a signature. Today for the first time I have received a signature without a text!"[2]

I also wonder whether Dr. Gomes's critic ever forgave him. I suspect not. When you are really right, secure in your superiority, what's to forgive?

There may be another element in the woman's indignation. As P. D. James has written in her *The Children of Men,* "It is difficult to be generous-minded to those we have greatly harmed." Even in my judgment of them!

Psalm 119:22, 23 can be read two ways. The actual meaning of the text is clear, because the second line parallels and clarifies the first:

Remove from me scorn and contempt, for I keep your statutes.

Though rulers sit together and slander me,
your servant will meditate on your decrees.

The psalmist has felt the stings of critics, the scorn of those who hold him in contempt. Please, God, protect me, he prays. Look at that first line again, though. *Remove from me* [my] *scorn and contempt, for I keep your statutes.* I would like to think that because I try to keep God's statutes—and because I know how far short I fall from perfect obedience—there would be no scorn and contempt in me. Yet how hard it is not to measure myself against others who seem to have fallen even farther—and to hold them in contempt for their weakness.

Forgiving

Every time I reread this incident I shake my head at the religious leaders. They feel no compunction in criticizing Jesus for forgiving the woman while they at the same time condemn her. They are scrupulous on the matter of forgiveness, insisting that only God has the right to forgive. Where are their scruples regarding condemning?

What bothers me about them is this: If you were to ask almost any critics of religion today what they base their criticism on, they would quickly tell you that it's the self-righteousness, the smug self-satisfaction coupled with the harsh judgmental spirit the religious exhibit toward those who don't agree with them or who violate their moral standards. Two thousand years after Christ, the scene plays out the same.

This becomes very personal for me. My own religious pilgrimage has been one toward a more open, accepting spirit. My sister and I were talking about this recently. We are enjoying a very satisfying friendship in our old age. Every now and then, though, she reminds me what a self-righteous prig I was as a youngster. I protest. Surely her memory is colored by the forgetfulness of the years. She insists. Secretly I know I should admit that she's right—but it's difficult to admit a flaw, even an old one, to your big sister.

In my reflective moments I marvel at God's inclusiveness and scold myself for mentally drawing lines between "us" and "them." I recall the Bible's golden text, memorized in my childhood but understood only in maturity: *"For God so loved the world that he gave his one and only Son, that whoever believes in him shall not perish but have eternal life"* (John 3:16). If ever there was an all-embracing statement, this is it. And the next verse opens the heart even wider:

"For God did not send his Son into the world to condemn the world, but to save the world through him."

We preachers sometimes sound as if we think Jesus came in order to condemn, not to save.

Remember Jesus' confrontation with the religious leaders who had dragged before Him a woman they claimed they caught in the act of adultery (John 8)? Even when I was young I thought, "Shame on them. What were they doing, spying? What's so virtuous about that?" The beautiful aspect of the story is the way Jesus shamed them into leaving the woman alone. Something about His tone of voice or the look in His eye made them conscious, perhaps as never before, of their own sinfulness. However He did it, He eventually found Himself alone with her (in itself a breach of social propriety). How safe she must have felt, finally.

Jesus straightened up and asked her, "Woman, where are they? Has no one condemned you?"

"No one, sir," she said.

"Then neither do I condemn you," Jesus declared. "Go now and leave your life of sin."

Scholars debate whether this passage should be in the Bible. It isn't found in the oldest manuscripts, so modern versions usually italicize it or print it as a footnote. I have yet to read a scholarly debate on whether the passage is true to what we know about Jesus, though. Scholars agree: pious types major in condemning; Jesus majors in giving people another chance.

Erma Bombeck comes to my assistance here. The gifted humorist, so adept at turning her human foibles into laughter fodder for the millions, said she learned a long time ago that if she took a crack at anyone but Adolf Hitler and herself she was in for a storm of criticism—or even a lawsuit.

She learned the lesson as a columnist. If she wanted her kind of writing to be accepted, she had to be kind to others. It's a lesson religious leaders could take to heart, don't you think?

Forgiven

What appears to be happening at Simon's dinner, at first reading? The woman doesn't belong in this home. She has pushed her way in, defying social convention. We would say she is making a spectacle of herself. But then, she has nothing to lose. Hers is the boldness of desperation.

Or, more accurately in this case, the boldness of forgiveness.

There is a deep root of courage, one not sufficiently appreciated by most of us religious people, we whose sins seem (to us) comparatively mild and whose corresponding sense of gratitude is therefore pretty shallow. That root is the assurance of being forgiven. The more you hate your sin, the more grateful, the more *boldly* grateful, you are toward the one who has forgiven you.

It is this sense of proportion that makes ingratitude so damnable—in the full meaning of the term. The ingrate can't forget self but rather forgets former favors; he makes his way by manipulation, always scouting, always looking for the best deal. Always anxious, ever quick to take offense at the slightest affront, equally alert to openings for self-advancement, the ingrate fears the loss of face or opportunity.

The grateful soul, on the other hand, can be almost oblivious to criticism, single-minded in devotion, determined to repay or at least to express appreciation. The boldness of this woman's action is striking, yet she remains strangely passive in the face of the criticism. She doesn't say a word. She doesn't have to. Her benefactor continues to defend her.

It isn't clear from the text whether Jesus had met her earlier and done some favor. Or has she come because of what she has heard about His miracles and compassion toward people like her? We don't know and we don't need to know. What comes through is the courage of the forgiven.

The power of forgiveness

In the wind down of the Gulf War (March 1991), our Mesa paper printed in bold type, "Schwarzkopf Offers

Apology." The story reported that the commanding general had apologized to President Bush for his "poor choice of words." He earlier told a television interviewer he had recommended that American troops press on to "annihilate" Iraqi forces. He implied he had disagreed with the White House on ending hostilities.

General Schwarzkopf then called a hastily arranged appearance at the U.S. military's press center to publicly apologize. He also reported that the president had called to tell him he still had "great confidence" in him.

The general explained that when President Bush found out how bad he was feeling because of the interpretation the media put on his comments, he telephoned Schwarzkopf. "And being the great man that he is, he called up to tell me to forget it."

What makes this story memorable to me is the fact that it was considered newsworthy in the first place. Is it so unusual that a man would regret what he said—or what the media said he said? And is it so remarkable that another man, even if he *is* the president, would call to cheer him up?

Unfortunately, the answer to both questions is yes. Forgiveness does not come easy; it's so rare it merits a headline.

And what a difference it makes to the forgiven!

At Hope International University we have been retelling a fascinating story I first heard when I bumped into Dr. Alan Rabe in the lobby of our office building. He was bursting with news. A professor of HopeOnLine and staff member with Food for the Hungry, Dr. Rabe goes on the Internet to teach his courses wherever he happens to be in the world. He had been working recently in Cambodia, he said, and while in Phnom Penh he picked up an English-language newspaper to read while eating in a nearby restaurant. On the front page was a full-color picture of a man called Duch, infamous in Cambodia as a henchman of the murderous Pol Pot, the evil genius of the killing fields that wiped out millions of Cambodians.

Duch's picture emblazoned the front page because he had

just done the unheard of: he had come out of hiding, the only one of Pol Pot's lieutenants to do so. He confessed his guilt (he personally oversaw the killing of fourteen thousand). He also admitted that he had become a Christian and was even then leading a Christian church he had started. He knew that his life would be endangered by this confession, but he had trusted his soul to God and was not afraid.

What caught Dr. Rabe's eye in the account that accompanied the picture was the name of our university. One of Hope's graduates, Christopher LaPel, minister of the Golden West Cambodian Christian Church in Los Angeles, goes to his homeland every year to conduct leadership seminars and evangelistic crusades. While on one of his annual trips there he had baptized Duch. He didn't know at the time who he was. He only knew that he was a sinner seeking a new life.

That Christopher was in Cambodia leading people to Christ (he has established three hundred fourteen new churches with more than twenty thousand members) is in itself remarkable. If anyone has a right to be bitter over the genocide, it is Christopher, who lost most of his family to Pol Pot's madness, killed by hands like Duch's. How was it possible, reporters later asked LaPel, for him to forgive and accept this man with so much of his family's blood on his hands?

Christopher quietly answers that he can't do otherwise. Christ has forgiven him. How can he withhold that forgiveness from anyone else, even Duch?

And what but Christ's forgiveness could have enticed Duch out of hiding? Where else could he have found the courage to go public, knowing that he most certainly will die? Jesus may forgive, and Christopher. But not the civil authorities.

"Cowards die many times; the brave never die but once." It's an old saying and, I suspect, true. But where do the brave get their courage? Is it genetic? Did someone teach them how to face danger without fear? We could debate at length and still not be sure we have exhausted the subject. But of this we may be certain: some people are brave because they have nothing to lose.

That is the case with Simon's unwanted guest. From Simon and his ilk she has nothing to gain and everything to lose. They offer her only scorn and rejection, no more in his house than anywhere else. They can't hurt her more than they already have.

From Jesus she has everything to gain. He offers her what no one else will. He forgives her.

How en-*courage*-ing.

---

[1]Gomes, Peter J. *Sermons*. New York: William Morrow & Co., 1998.

[2]Stott, John. *The Contemporary Christian*. Leicester, UK: Inter-Varsity Press, 1992.

GEAR UP

1. How is it possible to harm another person by judging him or her?

2. What do a critical spirit and a condemning spirit have in common?

3. When we criticize or judge others, what are we actually doing to ourselves?

4. How does a critical, judgmental spirit affect our spiritual growth?

5. What does God say about condemnation in Romans 8:1?

6. Why is it possible for those who have been forgiven to be more courageous than those who have been condemned?

7. Have you personally experienced the boldness of forgiveness? How does it give you confidence in your interactions with others?

8. How does the boldness of forgiveness give you confidence in your relationship with God (see Hebrews 4:16)?

9. Early in this study (page 115) Dr. Lawson wrote of "the bouquet of blessings" related to forgiveness. List the elements of this bouquet, then ask yourself, "Which of these do I need to spend time cultivating this week?"

10. How will you go about doing this?

11. Think of someone you need to forgive. Which of these blessings will you offer to that person this week?

12. How will you go about offering this blessing?

10
RESCUED FROM
DEATH

Matthew 27:15–28:20

IN EACH OF THE preceding chapters the mysterious and majestic hand of God has rescued the faithful from danger. The greatest rescue of all, against the greatest enemy of all—is Christ's deliverance from the tomb. I have saved the best for the last.

Jesus' resurrection is the core of the Christian faith, the essential fact upon which all else depends. Death could not hold Him down. He is risen, as He said. Take away the resurrection and you rob Christianity of its meaning. The apostle Paul declared, *If there is no resurrection of the dead, then not even Christ has been raised. And if Christ has not been raised, our preaching is useless and so is your faith* (1 Corinthians 15:13, 14). There would be nothing unique for us preachers to talk about, no credibility to what we say, if in the end Jesus was reduced to a corpse. His disciples would have gone back to their fishing and tax-collecting, mourning the loss of a good friend and mentor. For the rest of their lives they would reminisce about their glorious but futile adventure with Jesus, and that would have been the end of the matter.

But in fact God rescued Him.

After two thousand years theologians are still probing the significance of the *incarnation*, a wonderful Latinism meaning "in-the-flesh." John says in the prologue of his Gospel,

The Word [that was God] *became flesh and made his dwelling among us.* Nothing causes greater wonder, though, than that a man, this man, was more than man, was in fact Emmanuel, God with us. Jesus so completely identified with humanity that He even died like one of us.

Even in death, Jesus is one of us.

In the final pages of the Gospels, the Jesus we meet is not the bold teacher, the charismatic miracle worker, the amazing hero who dominates the pages of the New Testament. This Jesus is a convicted criminal, a human being alone in the night, enduring the awful isolation of dying, the almost universal sense of abandonment: *"My God, my God, why have you forsaken me?"*

We read of His death with recurring surprise every time we return to the scene. He who could have called ten thousand angels didn't. Dylan Thomas would have urged Him not to "go gentle into that good night" but instead to "rage, rage against the dying of the light." He does not rage; He does "go gentle." Before the guards and magistrates He seems strangely passive, nonresistant.

Bible students return to these pages (Matthew 27:15–28:20) again and again, drawn by the sheer contrast between the charismatic rabbi (cleansing the temple, healing the sick, and astonishing the crowds) and this submissive prisoner who, though He never leaves center stage, is more acted upon than acting. He lets Judas kiss Him though He sees through his treachery; He allows soldiers to hustle Him off to high priest and governor, (though their mockery had to sting); He endures the pain the executioners inflict as they hoist Him on the cross. He takes it all without protest.

He cries out to God, but not against us. *"Father, forgive them,"* He pleads, blaming ignorance rather than wickedness for our treachery. In the earlier part of the Gospels, we are in awe of His sheer brilliance and power. At His death, we applaud His quiet courage.

I said that even in death He is like us. What I should have said, in truth, is that He becomes what we would like to be.

This book about God's rescues has turned, even in this final study, into a series of profiles in courage. In each chapter except the preceding one, we have admired the bravery of the heroes we studied. They had to be rescued, but what valor they exhibited before they were delivered.

What strikes us as we read of Jesus' death is His unresisting acceptance of the inevitable. To fulfill His God-given mission, He has to die. As He identified with us in His birth and His baptism, so now He understands there can be no other-than-the-human-way back to His Father. He who is Son of God is also Son of Man, and as a man He must die. Emboldened by His sense of mission, He accepts every requirement of its fulfillment.

While I am writing these words about Jesus I can't get two of my dying friends out of my mind. Duane is in his mid-fifties, his powerful body withering under the assault of cancer. He is receiving the best medical treatment available, but weeks ago it became apparent that the best isn't good enough. Against the wishes of his physicians, Duane is home instead of in the hospital. His wife and stepson are caring for him around the clock. He has rejected any more chemotherapy. He refuses to return to the hospital. He wants no heroics performed on him. He has asked for his dialysis to be stopped. If you were to call in his home you would find him still in possession of his old poise. His jaw is set. You could read the pain in his eyes and you would miss the easy laughter of the past, but you would not catch a scent of fear.

He is going "gentle into that good night." He has lived with Christ; he will die with Him. Calmly. He is not afraid.

Gid is ninety years old. He wants to leave. Up until a few months ago his friends wondered at his robust good health. Then he fell, hitting the concrete sidewalk so hard his body was forced into shock. He has never recovered. If you were to visit him, he would tell you that he knows this is his last battle. He doesn't expect to recover. He doesn't want to.

"And why should I?" he demands to know. Gid gave his life to the Lord early in the twentieth century. He has served Him without a break ever since. He believes that after death comes the resurrection, as Jesus promised. Prolonged life on earth means more pain; his worn-out body has had it.

So Duane and Gid face their deaths with the courage Jesus taught us to muster—because of the life that lies beyond it.

As a whole, though, our society fears death. Someone has said *dead* is the new four-letter word. People don't die in our vocabulary. They pass away or go to sleep or become deceased or travel to the other side, as if our softened vocabulary can soften death's blow. There is something unreal about cemeteries now. Artificial turf and plastic clods cover the real dirt of the grave, and grave sites are garnished with plastic flowers that won't wilt, standing guard over the grave as a mute symbol of denial.

But in spite of the cosmetics, people still cry real tears over real dead bodies that are lowered into real dirt. The reality of death cannot be camouflaged. Jesus doesn't sidestep the issue. As one of us, He embraces His own death. He can do so because He trusts the One who governs both life and death.

He relies on the one in charge.

As we read the scriptural account of Jesus' death, one word keeps coming to mind, the name of what may well be the most important of spiritual attitudes. That word is *submission*. I spoke of friends Duane and Gid as if they are submitting to their inevitable deaths. That is not quite true. They can face death with such equanimity because long ago they submitted their lives to the one who is in charge.

British author John Mortimer's delightful creation Rumpole, English barrister, always refers to his wife as "she who must be obeyed." Not that Rumpole always obeys, you understand, but that she's that kind of wife.

Much more seriously, Duane and Gid believe God is "He

who must be obeyed," not because of compulsion but because of trust. They are not resisting death, because they believe their benevolent Father has willed it for their ultimate good. The doctors might think them a bit defiant. They have been known to rebel when instructed to obey this or that prescription. Respectfully but firmly they decline. They are obedient patients, but decided long ago who must be obeyed. God is the one in charge.

Our hometown newspaper for March 21, 1993, announced
> THERE'S NOBODY IN CHARGE OF DEATH IN ARIZONA
> FUNERAL BOARD CALLED INEFFECTIVE[1]

The subtitle explains the story; I copied the words because I found them funny. Of course there's someone in charge of death in Arizona. He just doesn't happen to have His office there.

The issue of control is a serious one, isn't it? Should Duane have the right to refuse chemotherapy? Should Gid be scolded for preparing to leave? I experienced something of their struggle when hit by a car many years ago. Even though my injuries were minor (broken arm and nose, superficial damage to face and legs), strangers immediately took over my life. I was forced to lie down on the pavement until the ambulance arrived, then lifted into it by paramedics, then required to remain on a gurney in the emergency room hallway. People kept on telling me everything to do until I finally escaped from the hospital ("checking out," they called it).

When I'm calling on fatally ill patients who have decided to take charge of their options, I sympathize. Though it isn't apparent at first, a closer reading of Jesus' death scenes yields this truth: Jesus is just allowing others to think they are in charge. He has previously decided to do whatever is necessary to complete the mission His Father gave Him. To the extent they are helping Jesus to that end, they can do what they want. But they cannot determine the outcome. Someone else is in charge.

He knows His mission is temporary.

Samuel Johnson reportedly said, "When a man knows he is going to be hanged in a fortnight, it concentrates his mind wonderfully." For many months Jesus has been preparing His disciples to face His crucifixion. He has labored with such intensity because His time was short. He did not fret over His impending doom, however, because He knew how much better life would be on the other side of the tomb.

In his *Life Preservers*, Bob Russell recounts how Paul Azinger faced up to the brevity of his life. The popular golf professional had just won the 1993 PGA championship and had ten tournament victories to his credit when his cancer was discovered. Lying in an X-ray room as the technician adjusted the machines, he became genuinely afraid. The reality hit: he could die from cancer. But then another truth hit him even harder. He was going to die eventually anyway. The question wasn't whether, but when.

"In that same moment, something Larry Moody, the man who leads our Bible study on the PGA tour, had said to me many times came to mind. 'Zinger, we're not in the land of the living going to the land of the dying. We're in the land of the dying going to the land of the living.'" When Paul came to this realization, he said that nothing else, even his championship and ten victories, mattered.[2]

The apostle Paul faced up to the same reality. Here is his response:

Therefore we do not lose heart. Though outwardly we are wasting away, yet inwardly we are being renewed day by day (2 Corinthians 4:16).

This is the difference. Bodies must decay; persons do not have to. In Christ there is ongoing renewal. Jesus' body would die on the cross, His divine assignment at an end, but the tomb isn't the end of His story.

He knows His body is temporary.

During my few days in Maui on Brian's windsurfing excursion, I spent most of my time at the computer working on this book. But I still had time to glance up occasionally. When the wind is blowing and the sails are taut, windsurfing is a magnificent spectator sport. On closer inspection, however, when the sailors are quitting for the day, hauling their equipment across the lawn to storage, the spectacle of the sport is spoiled. Instead of the panorama of symmetrical vessels gracefully racing across the waters, here is an unappetizing motley of drenched windsurfers. Tall ones and short ones; young, lithe bodies and, wrinkly ones with varicose veins. No really fat ones, admittedly, but several shades of thin. What you don't find here are many drop-dead photo models. These men and women are into exercising, hard physical workouts, careful dieting and other regimes to toughen themselves, but one truth comes across at the day's end: no amount of physical exercise can save them from the ravages of time.

One of the men staying in our house, for example, was a pretty impressive fifty-one-year-old. The man has done it all, or almost all: motocross racing, ocean kayaking, and bodybuilding are numbered among his achievements. He was in Hawaii to learn windsurfing, and he did very well. As I said, a pretty impressive fifty-one. But not an impressive twenty-one. The years are taking their toll, even on this athlete. He is now not what he has been before.

About aging, it has been said, there are three types of people:

Those who were born with handicaps

Those who have developed handicaps through injury or aging

And those living in temporarily healthy bodies.

Note the "temporarily." Thus the apostle Paul writes (in 2 Corinthians 5:2, 4, 8), *We groan, longing to be clothed with our heavenly dwelling. . . . We do not wish to be unclothed but to be clothed with our heavenly dwelling. . . . We . . .*

would prefer to be away from the body and at home with the Lord. If we don't agree with Paul when we are thirty-five, we will when we are sixty-five or ninety-five.

I recently spoke at an Arizona church. Following the service an old friend greeted me. Not having seen him for over a year, I was not prepared for the meeting. In fact, at first I didn't recognize him. Badly bent, he labored toward me, leaning heavily on his crutches, making barely discernible progress with each mini step, his face contorted with effort and pain. The energy that marked his brisk walk of a year ago was gone. He groaned, and as a man of lifelong faith, he let me know he was longing to be "at home with the Lord" and away from his miserable body. He has lived on this earth many more years than Jesus did. His mission was of longer duration than Jesus' was, but his, too, is coming to an end.

He knows He has not lived in vain.

On that trip to India I mentioned earlier, Joy and I visited Dolly Chitwood's grave. Leah Moshier, her longtime partner in the Kulpahar Kids' Home, stood beside us as we read her headstone noting her forty-nine years of service in rural India. We had just left a church service where I spoke to more than two hundred boys and girls of the nearly one thousand these devoted women rescued from death and raised as their own children. Leah herself is now over eighty. She still presides over this remarkable mission, but she, too, knows her time is limited. We talked for a while of what a remarkable ministry she and Dolly have had. Dolly died knowing she had not lived in vain.

It's a good feeling. Jesus died with the same knowledge.

After John Lennon was fatally shot, a fan pointed out, "The music didn't die. Only the man did."[3] As we stood in that Indian cemetery, the music of the worship lingered in our heads. Only the physical Dolly had died; the music of her life is still being replayed in the lives of her children.

Many years ago G. K. Chesterton reported seeing in a newspaper article that a man was enlisting as a soldier in Portsmouth. Some form was put before him to be filled out, asking among other things what his religion was. He wrote down, "Methuselahite." When asked to explain, he said it was his religion "to live as long as he could," like the oldest man in the Bible. Chesterton wisely commented that the soldier "formed one word that defines the paganism of today."[3]

Chesterton flourished in the early years of the twentieth century. What would he say of today's worship at the altars of longevity? With each passing decade the children born to that period enjoy a longer life expectancy, enjoy it, and demand even more. There is talk that in the twenty-first century an average lifespan of one hundred twenty years (in developed countries) is reachable.

We welcome this development, provided a certain quality of life can be maintained. What concerns us, though, is the growing belief that life is to be measured only by the quantity of years and not the quality of contribution. For the Methuselahite, life consists of postponing death as long as possible. But one day death's turn will come. What then? If the significance of life consists only in the accumulation of days in the body, then death must be the final and awful defeat.

If, on the other hand, we have lived for others (using Christ as our example), then death can be welcomed as a much-earned rest and pathway to reward beyond the grave. I understand that rabbis often end a memorial service with, "May his memory be for a blessing." It's a beautiful benediction, but it can have real meaning only when the deceased has first lived as a blessing. And no one blesses by merely living a long time. Methuselah is noted in the Bible for one thing only: he lived a very long time. Nothing else is remembered. His memory blesses no one.

Memories of Jesus, however, have blessed the remembering for two thousand years. He did not live in vain.

His trust in the Father is vindicated.

After the Sabbath, at dawn on the first day of the week, Mary Magdalene and the other Mary went to look at the tomb.

There was a violent earthquake, for an angel of the Lord came down from heaven and, going to the tomb, rolled back the stone and sat on it. His appearance was like lightning, and his clothes were white as snow. The guards were so afraid of him that they shook and became like dead men.

The angel said to the women, "Do not be afraid, for I know that you are looking for Jesus, who was crucified. He is not here; he has risen, just as he said."

. . . .

"*After three days I will rise again,*" He said (Matthew 27:63). And He did, just as He said.

He then began to teach them that the Son of Man must suffer many things and be rejected by the elders, chief priests and teachers of the law, and that he must be killed and after three days rise again (Mark 8:31). And He did, just as He said.

Jesus took the Twelve aside and told them, "We are going up to Jerusalem, and everything that is written by the prophets about the Son of Man will be fulfilled. He will be handed over to the Gentiles. They will mock him, insult him, spit on him, flog him and kill him. On the third day he will rise again" (Luke 18:31-33). And He did, just as He said.

Jesus said to her [Martha], *"I am the resurrection and the life. He who believes in me will live, even though he dies; and whoever lives and believes in me will never die"* (John 11:25, 26). And it will be so, just as He said.

[1]*Mesa Tribune,* 1/12/81.
[2]Russell, Bob. *Life Preservers.* Cincinnati: Standard Publishing Co., 1997.
[3]Chesterton, G. K., *The Man Who Was Chesterton.* Manchester, NH: Ayer Company Publishers, Inc., 1977.

140 *Rescued!*

GEAR UP

1. Which events in Matthew 27:15–28:20 do you return to most often?

2. What impact has this event made on your life?

3. What does Jesus' prayer, *"Father, forgive them, for they do not know what they are doing"* (Luke 23:34), reveal about the heart of God?

4. What impact has His prayer made on your own thinking?

5. What are some of the fears people have about death?

6. Which of these fears are most real to you?

7. What difference has the resurrection made in your ability to face the reality of death?

8. Does knowing that God is in charge of the hour of your death give you peace? Why, or why not?

9. How does Larry Moody's statement, "We're in the land of the dying going to the land of the living" affect your perspective of death and dying?

10. How does living each day in obedience to Him ensure that we will not have lived in vain?

11. What choices do you need to make today to ensure that your life will have meaning?

12. Think about your life. What do you want people to remember about you?